What Others Are Saying About *A Community Called Taizé*

"If a virtual reality tour can be conducted through words, Jason Brian Santos has done it in this book, giving the reader a sense that she has now visited Taizé and is eager to go again—but this time in the flesh. Along the way, Jason helps us to understand why this movement of reconciliation has attracted thousands of young people all over the world and encourages us to learn from the brothers ways in which this same spirit can infect Christians from all branches of the splintered church."

Dennis Okholm, professor of theology, Azusa Pacific University, and author of *Monk Habits for Everyday People*

"Having been to Taizé several times, I know what a spellbinding place it is. I also know how extremely difficult it would be to capture the beauty and mystery of the place and its people with words on a page. That's why Jason Santos's achievement is so noteworthy. What he has done with *A Community Called Taizé* is to write both a primer on that wonderful community and a pilgrim's love story. I highly commend this book to those who've been to Taizé, those who wish to go and even those who've sung a Taizé chant in worship. All will be blessed by this book."

Tony Jones, author of *The Sacred Way: Spiritual Practices for Everyday Life* and *The New Christians: Dispatches from the Emergent Frontier*

"A very helpful guide to Taizé for thoughtful seekers, especially young people. Animated by the warm and respectful spirit of a fellow traveler, this practical and appreciative introduction can serve as a very good starting point for someone who desires to learn more about the popular Taizé songs and place them in their context, or someone thinking of visiting this unique community."

Elsie McKee, Archibald Alexander Professor of Reformation Studies and the History of Worship, Princeton Theological Seminary

"Jason Brian Santos's introduction quite literally took my breath away. Wow! Santos's description of the rhythms, values, philosophy and theology of the Taizé community should be read by anyone longing to cultivate an authentic Christian community."

Mike King, president of YouthFront, pastor of Jacob's Well Church, Kansas City, and author of *Presence-Centered Youth Ministry*

"Jason Brian Santos has caught the essence of the Taizé community through his scholarly, perceptive and spiritual presentation. In an amazing style, this book provides a real taste of Taizé for the benefit of those who have not yet undertaken a pilgrimage there. Jason provides insightful, practical and powerful tools for everyone who would like to undertake a pilgrimage to Taizé. Through his own experiences and his scholarly articulation, he helps others serve themselves to the richness of Christian spirituality and spirit of ecumenism that permeate the world through the hills of Burgundy that nestle the community of Taizé."

Bishop Sudarshana Devadhar, resident bishop, New Jersey area,
The United Methodist Church

"*A Community Called Taizé* is a jewel of a book, like Taizé itself—simple, reverent and surprisingly comprehensive. With effortless prose, Jason Santos makes us feel like we are there, taking part in the community's monastic rhythms, singing the prayers, meeting the brothers (and some women too). Santos has thought of everything, from local customs to packing lists—but don't miss the last part of the book, which suggests what churches can learn from the community's theology, practices and prayers. If you are visiting Taizé—or if you simply wonder why an ecumenical community of brothers attracts more than 100,000 young people every year without a single ice-breaker—you simply must read this book. It will set the standard for our understanding of Taizé for years to come."

Kenda Creasy Dean, author of *Practicing Passion: Youth and the Quest for a Passionate Church*

A Community Called
TAIZÉ

A Story of Prayer, Worship and Reconciliation

Jason Brian Santos

Foreword by Desmond Tutu

271
. 8
S237

IVP Books

An imprint of InterVarsity Press
Downers Grove, Illinois

InterVarsity Press
P.O. Box 1400, Downers Grove, IL 60515-1426
World Wide Web: www.ivpress.com
Email: email@ivpress.com

Design: Cindy Kiple

All photographs (including cover photograph) taken by the author.

ISBN 978-0-8308-3525-6

Printed in the United States of America ∞

Library of Congress Cataloging-in-Publication Data

Santos, Jason Brian.

 A community called Taizé: a story of prayer, worship, and
 reconciliation / Jason Brian Santos; foreword, Desmond Tutu.
  p. cm.
 Includes bibliographical references.
 ISBN 978-0-8308-3525-6 (pbk.: alk. paper)
 1. Communauté de Taizé. I. Title.
 BV4408.S26 2008
 271'.8—dc22

                                                                              2008022657

P 25 24 23 22 21 20 19 18 17 16 15 14 13 12 11 10 9 8 7 6 5 4 3 2 1

Y 29 28 27 26 25 24 23 22 21 20 19 18 17 16 15 14 13 12 11 10 09 08

To the Brothers of Taizé

for trusting me in this endeavor

Contents

A Word from the Taizé Community

Jason Santos shares with us, in extensive detail and with personal involvement, his experience as a visitor to our hill in Burgundy. His hope—and ours as well—is that it may allow North Americans to see that, beyond the repetitive chanting and a particular style of meditative prayer, Taizé is an ecumenical monastic community that wishes, through worship and community life, to help young adults discover Jesus Christ as a source of reconciliation for divided Christians and as a promise of peace in the human family.

Brother John, Taizé

Foreword

During my time as Secretary General of the South African Council of Churches, South Africa was on a knife edge. In June 1976, many young people had been killed by the police, but despite that, they continued to display hope and courage in the face of state repression.

On a visit to Taizé in 1979, during worship in the Church of Reconciliation and surrounded by five thousand young people from all quarters of the globe, I received a vision. I imagined a pilgrimage of young South Africans of all races coming to Taizé to worship, to laugh, to love, to rough it together as a foretaste of our faith in a nonracial South Africa. A number was given—144, from the 144,000 in Revelation 7.

I discussed this with Brother Roger, and the vision became reality. I was sad to have been prevented from going on this pilgrimage, since my passport was withheld by the South African government. But the young people went, and this made me overflow with joy.

I am told that the bells rang out over the village of Taizé when our pilgrimage of hope arrived at this "little Springtime." In my language, I would call it a place of *Ubuntu,* a place of community, where every single person matters and where no one is diminished since that would lead to the diminishment of all.

We have never tried to calculate the effect that the 1980 visit had on the young people or on South Africa, but the fact that they were pilgrims to a place of reconciliation meant that this had a tremendous impact on the life of the whole group, many of whom are now in leadership positions, faithfully serving the church and civil society.

Of course many other young South Africans followed, and over the last twenty-eight years the relationship between Taizé and Africa has grown significantly. Africa is the place where crucifixion and resurrection find their deepest meaning, and where building trust and reconciliation is an ongoing daily reality. Recent events in South Africa have showed us the amount of work that still needs to be done to even build trust between the different peoples who make up the continent of Africa. I have always said that we are all children of God and that in Christ there is no Rwandese or Congolese, there is no Burundian or Kenyan, no Nigerian or South African: we are all one in Christ Jesus. I know that this is the message that the Taizé community also proclaims and that they are in solidarity with us as we press this message home in South Africa, across the whole continent of Africa and in the rest of the world where "fear of the stranger" still needs to be turned into friendship and reconciliation and trust.

Jason Santos, the author of this book, has done us all a tremendous service by carefully and beautifully explaining both the practical realities of being at Taizé and its inner spiritual realities. It is my prayer that as more and more people read this book, it will strengthen the work of building trust and reconciliation in the world amongst all God's people. Through the faith of the young and the friendships they continue to build amongst themselves, we are being shown a glimpse of the kingdom, and this book can only contribute to the nurturing of the seeds of trust being sown by the community of brothers at Taizé.

God bless you.

Archbishop-emeritus Desmond Mpilo Tutu
June 1, 2008, Cape Town, South Africa

Preface

I have always wanted to write books. For as long as I can remember, book ideas would come to me at the most random times. The topics ranged from various practices of spirituality to, believe it or not, a novel about a poker-playing seminarian (nonautobiographical, of course). Despite this desire of mine, when I first visited Taizé I never anticipated writing a book on the community. As my academic research on Taizé grew, however, I found myself thinking, *Someone really should write something about the community and how their chants are used in other contexts.*

After my second research trip, I wrote an email to one of the brothers, sheepishly suggesting that perhaps I might be a good person to write about the community for an English-speaking context. I offered the brothers my ideas and assured them that I wouldn't undertake this project without their blessing.

Weeks went by before an email arrived in my inbox from one of my contact brothers. Much to my surprise, not only had they unanimously decided that the book was a good idea, they also felt that I was the right person to write it. I remember reading the email with emotions that ranged from excitement to disbelief. How could a community as significant as Taizé trust a thirty-three-year-old doctoral student—whom they barely knew—to represent them to a North American and English-speaking context? Up to that point, I had only published one article about the community and written two academic papers on my research. I wasn't a known researcher, nor had I really proven myself to be a good writer.

As I write this, the measure of trust they have afforded me in this endeavor still bewilders me. After digging significantly deeper into the ethos and rhythm of their community, I am convinced that this trust is not of human origin, but one enabled by the Holy Spirit. Just as God trusts us to be coworkers for his kingdom, the brothers found it in their hearts to trust me. Perhaps it's not even trust in me as a person but rather the fact that they have simply trusted God with their lives, their community and the manner in which the world perceives them. Maybe when we truly trust God we are empowered to trust others, because the outcome of our trust—for better or for worse—is in God's providential hands. In any case, it was with a profound sense of being unquestionably trusted that I undertook the task of writing this book.

Those who know me well were probably glad when this project started coming to a close, because for over two years, many of my academic discussions and dinner-party conversations turned toward the Taizé community. While some have accused me of having an infatuation with the community, I know that it goes far deeper than that. Having been spiritually formed through several denominations ranging from conservative evangelicalism to mainline Protestantism, I've seen a fairly full palate of what the North American ecclesial landscape has to offer. I've been on and led a dozen or so mission trips, I spent the summers of my teen years in Christian camps, and I pretty much grew up in my local church. To date, I've spent eleven years in higher theological education working out my understanding of faith. In fact, I can't really imagine my life without the influence of Christian theology and the church at large. Yet, in the midst of all of my theological studies and spiritual formation, something inside of me awoke during my first two weeks in Taizé. Although that first exposure to the community was transformational, my further research on Taizé made the community more and more significant to my spiritual pilgrimage.

As a person who can put most things I think into words, there still exists something—some quality about the community—that words fail to capture. I know that what I'm saying borders on hagiography, but my own inability to formulate in precise words my experience with the community has been echoed through dozens upon dozens of interviews and conversations with young people. Without question, there is something different about Taizé. Although most of the time I feel like I can't quite put my finger on it, in the pages that follow I'll make a valiant attempt to describe the community through my own encounter with it and through the stories and experiences of hundreds of young people.

Using my own experience as a starting point, I'll share with you how my first two weeks in the community changed my understanding of trust and reconciliation. Following this, I will attempt to immerse you in a simulated encounter with Taizé by walking you through what you might experience if you were to actually visit the community for a day. I should warn you that at times you may feel a bit like you're on a guided tour, but in the end, you'll get a fairly accurate portrayal of the experience. My hope is that I'll provide you with enough information about the community to pique your interest into how and why Taizé has become such a significant place in the lives of literally hundreds of thousands of young people across the world.

Next, I'll take you for a short jaunt through the community's history before we look at the life of the brothers and of those who help them welcome so many young pilgrims each year. Then we'll explore the development of the prayers and I'll propose some key qualities that have shaped the ethos of the community. Ultimately, I will suggest some things we can learn from the Taizé community and ways we can more faithfully use their chants in our own prayer gatherings.

It's also worth noting that there are three appendices in this book. Appendix A should prove helpful if you're planning or thinking about planning a trip to the community. It touches on everything from what to pack to how to get there. In appendix B, you'll find the "life commitment" vows that each brother takes when he decides that God has called him to a monastic life. Then in appendix C I have included a list of books and other resources that will prove helpful if you're interested in learning more about Taizé. Finally, I have also included in the back matter a short glossary of terms and locations that are particular to the community. It's there for your convenience, so refer to it as needed.

I really hope that this is only the beginning of your interest in the Taizé community, not because the world needs more Taizé groupies running around, but because if my experience proves even remotely applicable to other spiritual seekers, this community has something significant to teach us all. With that in mind, I encourage you to allow yourself to be transformed by the pages that follow—not by my words, but by the spirit of an amazing community that shines through them.

1

My Pilgrimage to Taizé

Bless the Lord, my soul, and bless God's holy name.
Bless the Lord, my soul, who leads me into life.

⌔

There have only been two times in my life when I've had what I consider a legitimate surreal experience.[1] Not just a dreamy sort of surrealism that people associate with strange or highly unique experiences, but the type of surrealism where you have to stop and ask yourself, "Is this really real . . . or am I dreaming?" The first occurred in New York City in 1995. A few friends from college and I spent the day in the city and ended up right in the middle of Times Square for the famous "Dick Clark's New Year's Rockin' Eve" countdown. Suffice it to say, when that clock struck twelve and they dropped several tons of confetti from the skyscrapers above, I legitimately didn't know whether I was dreaming or if what I was experiencing was actually happening. I remember looking up into the sky and throwing my hands straight up toward the falling multicolored flurry of paper snow (like in the movies), which ultimately blanketed over 200,000 merrymakers that night. It was one of those moments where the boundaries between reality and fantasy were unquestionably blurred.

The second surreal experience happened the night that a mentally unstable Romanian woman murdered Brother Roger, the founder and prior of the Taizé community, during the evening prayers. What made the event surreal for me was not any special personal connection to Brother Roger or to the community but rather the fact that I was sitting about ten meters away from Brother Roger when it happened. Even more, it was my first evening in Taizé and my first time attending the prayers. But before I get too far into this story, let me back up and fill in a few preliminary details about how I ended up in Taizé that night.

For some time, I had known about Taizé, and both my wife, Shannon, and I had wanted to make a pilgrimage to the community. During the time I was working as a youth minister at the American Protestant Church in Bonn, Germany, we tried to arrange a trip several times, but Taizé is not easy to get to, even from western Germany. To complicate the planning more, our son, Judah, was two years old at the time, which made the trip seem even more challenging. At that time in our lives, the trip just never came together.

A couple of years later, while working on a Master's of Divinity degree at Princeton Theological Seminary, I decided to create an independent study on the community, primarily focusing on the question, "Why do young people go to Taizé?"

After receiving a few generous donations that would enable me to spend two weeks in the community, I booked my flight for the last two weeks of August 2005. When the fifteenth of August came, I packed my backpack and flew out. Like most transatlantic flights that depart in the evening and rob you of a good night's sleep, mine was long and tiresome. To top it all off, I left the United States with a bad head cold that decided to punish me in the middle of the flight by making my ears feel like they were bleeding. It was horrendous.

Nevertheless, when I arrived in Charles de Gaulle International Airport in Paris my adrenaline kicked in and I was ready to continue my journey by land. After an hour-long bus ride to the Gare de Lyon train station, I faced the challenge of purchasing a train ticket to Mâcon-Loché, the train station where I could catch a bus to Taizé. There I was, exhausted, unable to hear anything, yelling in English at the top of my voice that I wanted a ticket to "MA-CONE . . . NO . . . MA-CONE . . . IT'S NEAR TAY-ZAY . . . I SAID, TAY-ZAY!" Eventually, with only a few disgusted French onlookers still glaring at me, I succeeded in procuring my passage. In the process, however, I unfortunately discovered that my TGV high-speed train wouldn't leave for another three hours. So I decided to use the time to collect a few essentials: a phone card, a few bottles of water, fruit, cheese and a baguette. I was relieved that I didn't need much French for these transactions—just point and pay.

When the time finally came for my train to leave, I was more than ready to continue my journey. After a two-hour train ride, I found myself in Mâcon-Loché with yet another hour to wait for the bus. By the time it picked me up, I felt quite weary and longed for nothing more than a good night's rest. Despite the beauty of the rolling hills of France's Burgundy region, between the warmth of the sun beaming through the windows and the soothing vibrations of the bus I found myself nodding off in a dreamy state of exhaustion. Before long, I heard the bus driver announce the Gare Taizé stop. Much to my surprise, I was the only one exiting the bus at the stop at the bottom of the hill. (Later I discovered there was a second stop that drops you off right in front of the welcome building.) Disoriented from my dozing and slightly confused, I trudged up the hill to the entrance of the community. I had finally arrived.

I was immediately welcomed by a young German girl who was kind enough to offer me some cold fruit tea and some sort of bread, which was a bit reminiscent of Christmas fruitcake. Because dinner was about to start (it was almost 7:00 p.m.), she rushed me through my welcome orientation and handed me a meal ticket and map, on which she circled in red the dormitory where I would be sleeping, the tent where I could collect my meals and the most important building in Taizé—the Church of Reconciliation. She sent me on my way with just enough time to drop my belongings off in my dor-

Village from the bottom of the hill

mitory (in which I was the only occupant at the time) and hurry over to the adult tent for a meal. After a simple but filling meal, I washed up and made my way to the church for evening prayers. I wanted to be a little early to try to find a good place to sit. Little did I know that my eagerness would ultimately situate me within view of a tragedy that I will never forget for the rest of my life.

One by one fellow pilgrims packed into the church as the brothers, wearing their white prayer robes, quietly took their places in the center of the church. I was maybe thirty feet from where Brother Roger was sitting. With bleary eyes and the Taizé songbook in hand, I fumbled my way into the first chant. Just as I was settling into the melody of this chant I heard a piercing, blood-curdling scream come from the center of the church. I whipped my head up just in time to see a brother cloaked in a white prayer robe lunge toward a woman who was next to Brother Roger.

Within a few seconds, most of the twenty-five hundred sojourners present that night stood to their feet in an attempt to catch a glimpse of what caused such an audible disturbance. A minute later, however, several of the volunteers were asking everyone to sit down and continue praying. No matter how hard I tried, I couldn't regain focus on the prayers right away. Having grown up in the Pentecostal tradition, my first thought was that the woman who screamed was demon-possessed. It took several minutes for the church to settle as there were several brothers still moving about, but eventually it did. I was finally able to reenter the prayers, albeit with some lingering uncertainty as to the event that transpired only moments ago.

Then, around 9:30, one of the brothers stepped up to the lectern, turned the microphone on and began speaking in French. I had no idea what he was saying, but I knew it wasn't good. The next few minutes felt like an hour. One by one, faces of shock and terror emerged on the landscape of the crowded church. I could hear pockets of young girls bursting into tears. Questions flooded my mind. *Did the young woman die? Did someone get hurt?* The horrible sinking feeling that deepened in my stomach was only confirmed when the brother finally concluded his words in French and spoke in English. The only words he said that I can remember were, "Brother Roger is dead." Question after question raced through my mind. *What happened? Who was that woman? Did she hurt Brother Roger? Did he have a heart attack?* I felt as if I were truly dreaming—it was utterly surreal. *This can't be happening . . . not here . . . not now.* I don't remember leaving the church that night, but I do remember hundreds of crying young people talking in other languages on their cell phones.

I didn't know anyone who spoke English and I had no idea what was going on. On the way back to my dormitory, I stopped by the public phones hoping to call my wife, Shannon, and tell her that I had arrived safely as well as what had just happened to Brother Roger. Since the lines to the phones were several people deep and growing, I decided to retire for the evening. As I entered my dimly lit dormitory, a chill of eeriness crept up my spine with the realization that I was going to have to spend the night alone in my empty dorm room with no lock on the door, after the prior of Taizé died unexpectedly in the church. I felt very alone indeed.

I ended up returning to the public phones and calling Shannon before going to bed. It was comforting to hear her voice and to know that she would be praying that night. But not surprisingly, I didn't sleep much, quickly sitting up in my bunk at even the tiniest sound that came from outside the door. The footsteps passing outside my room were plentiful that night; I presume I wasn't the only one who had a rough time falling asleep.

Eventually, of course, the sun did rise. After my normal morning rituals, I ran into a young Korean American from San Francisco—finally, someone

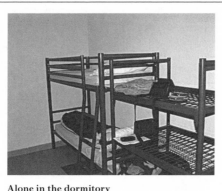

Alone in the dormitory

who spoke English. Much to my dismay, however, he gave me an extremely detailed description about what had really happened the previous night, as he had been sitting only about five feet away from Brother Roger. The details he offered are far too gruesome to fully share, but the short of it was this: he saw the woman approach Brother Roger, whisper something to him and pull out a knife. Then she started stabbing at his throat. His testimony confirmed the unthinkable: Brother Roger was murdered.

Needless to say, I was shocked. I could hardly believe someone would take the life of such a humble and gentle man. Bit by bit throughout the day more information surfaced about the murder. The woman was Romanian. She had been to Taizé a few years earlier and had wanted to meet with Brother Roger. She was unsuccessful. In Romania, she had a history of disrupting worship services through abrupt screaming. As it turns out, she was actually asked to leave Taizé three times prior to the incident. No one was quite sure why she had returned to Taizé this time. Apparently, she had purchased the knife earlier that day in a little shop in Cluny (a neighboring town that is quite significant to Western monasticism). The French police took her into custody that evening, and for the next few days there were cameras and news reporters everywhere, filming the pilgrims eating, working and praying. In fact, it wasn't until after Brother Roger's funeral a week later that everything seemed to settle down.

This was how my pilgrimage to Taizé began. When I entered the village that first evening, I had no connections to the community, the brothers or Brother Roger; however, when I left Taizé two weeks later, I felt as though I would be linked to the community forever.

Over the past two years I have returned to Taizé for research a couple of times, I have led prayers using the Taizé chants with a small group of Princeton University students, and I also began teaching about the community in colleges, at conferences and on retreats. In these encounters, I have had the opportunity to speak with hundreds of people about Taizé, both those who have made pilgrimages there and those who have experienced the chants in their local churches and parishes. Through these exchanges, consequently, I have come to realize that many Christians who use the Taizé chants in their own worship have very little understanding about the community in which the chants were birthed. This, as a matter of fact, became the primary impetus for my writing this book—to expose worship leaders, pastors, college and university students, and laity who have never been to Taizé to the community of brothers behind the chants. In these pages you will not only gain a glimpse into the communal life, the liturgy and the unspoken ethos of the Taizé community, but you will also be able to glean why and how the prayers have grown and spread throughout the world.

This is how I would ask you, the reader, to frame the rest of this book: as a window into the life of a community that understands itself as the starting point for young pilgrims. What follows in the chapters to come is a description of a community that is living out the gospel message in a radically different way. They live a lifestyle that may confront, challenge and inspire you beyond your expectations. In the end, you may want to visit Taizé or you may not. The goal of this book is not to draw more tourism to a little village in the Burgundy region of France—they definitely don't want that—but to draw you into the life of a community of brothers whose very existence stands as a witness to the unity and truth of the gospel. As a North American who grew up in a culture devoid of any real notion of pilgrimage or monasticism, I have gleaned a wealth of knowledge and wisdom from the Taizé community. My hope is that you will too.

2

Welcome to Taizé

I am sure I shall see the goodness of the Lord in the land of the living.
Yes, I shall see the goodness of our God, hold firm, trust in the Lord.

◯

My first twenty-four hours in Taizé during that first pilgrimage were, thankfully, very atypical for the community. So what does a normal week there look like? If your only exposure to the Taizé community has been through a song or two in your church's weekly liturgy or in a local prayer service, think of this chapter as a bird's-eye view into the daily rhythm of life of many of the pilgrims that visit there. For those of you who have visited the community one or more times, let this chapter be a short jaunt down memory lane. You might learn something new as well. I'm willing to bet there are a handful of stories and bits of information that will surprise even the most seasoned Taizé pilgrim.

As we look at a day in this unique community, allow me to offer one caveat: change is quite common in Taizé. The changes range from subtle adaptations that only the keenest eye will notice (such as a lighter coat of paint on the back wall of the chancel area), to overt changes that everyone notices (like the integration of their new red bowls in 2006). If you haven't been to Taizé in recent years, changes that have taken place since Brother Roger's death might prompt you to say, "That's not what it was like when I was there."

Alternatively, if you're planning a trip to the community, you might find that subtle changes have taken place since the publication of this book. In fact, I can almost guarantee it; with only six months between my last two visits to the community, I noticed half a dozen changes that took me by surprise. Change and adaptation are a part of the ethos of Taizé—and you'll begin to see why this is the case. With that said, the rhythm of the *communal* life is fairly established, so these next few pages should portray an accurate portrait of that aspect of the life of the community not just now but for years to come.

ACCUEIL A TAIZÉ

Imagine that you've just arrived in the community after fifteen hours of travel.[1] You're exhausted and want nothing more than a hot shower and a warm meal. The bus doors squeak open and you step out onto a dusty paved road edged by earth on both sides. You drag your forty-pound backpack out of the belly of the bus and turn toward a square, ranch-style building with a large extended awning that offers considerable shade to an as-

sortment of long wooden benches. To your right sits the tiny village of Taizé with its quaint, picturesque houses and winding paths. To your left is the main road that leads both in and out of Taizé. It's lined by neatly trimmed five-foot hedges on both sides.

The hedge-lined road

As you look forward again, you notice a sign hanging on the side of the ranch-style building that reads "Accueil Welcome" (*accueil* means "reception" or "welcome" in French). You tiredly walk toward the doors of the building; it's called Casa, which literally means "house" in Spanish. Casa is Taizé's official welcome house.

All of the significant buildings in Taizé have names, in part because of an old tradition and also simply because Brother Roger liked them to have names. Over the years, many of the buildings have undergone several name changes in order to make them easier to pronounce for the ever-diversifying pilgrim population. Naming the buildings both helps newcomers orient themselves in the community and creates a familiar environment for everyone who visits.

While the brothers could have called Casa "The Welcome Center," *Casa* aims at conveying a more hospitable sentiment, one that says, "Come into our home." Indeed, the feeling of welcome at Taizé echoes the oft-used phrase, "Mi casa es su casa."[2] Each week, the brothers convey to thousands and thousands of pilgrims who come through Casa's doors, "Welcome to Taizé. Our home is your home."

Casa

As you enter the simple stucco walls of Casa, you find a dozen young people and a few brothers waiting to greet you with cold tea and a cookie or sweet bread of some variety. A young person saying "Welcome to Taizé" is your confirmation that you've finally arrived. Your journey to the village is finally over, even though your pilgrimage has just begun. After you finish your snack, the welcome team seats you on a simple bench with several other pilgrims (presumably who speak the same language), and a member of the week's welcome team joins you.[3] Even if you've been to the community before, the brothers still desire that each pilgrim be welcomed by a young person. This young person could be either male or female and may be from another country. He or she might not even speak English as their first language. (In all the times I've visited Taizé, I've never had a native English speaker welcome me.) It's their job for the week to explain the rhythm of life that characterizes Taizé, to provide you with a welcome pamphlet (on which there is a map of the community) and to answer your questions.

Once your orientation is over, the young person sends you to the meal and contributions table where you pay for your meal ticket and lodging for the week. Your ticket is a small paper card with the various meals for each day of the week. As you file through the meal lines, someone will mark the appropriate meal off with a marker. It's not a perfect system, but it does successfully provide over one million meals a year. The amount you pay for your meals and lodging during your stay is quite flexible. In order to determine how much you should pay, they first consider your country of origin, because the system operates on a sliding scale. For example, people from the United Kingdom contribute more for the week than people from countries in Africa. They also adjust your contribution based on how long you are staying and whether or not you are sleeping in their dormitories or if you brought your own tent or camper. If you're a young person (under thirty years old), your costs are considerably less as well. After all these factors are considered, they present to you a contribution range with a minimum and a maximum amount you can pay. At that point, what you contribute within that range is completely up to you. By all calculations, Taizé is probably one of the least expensive places to stay in France. For a young person it's less than ten dollars a night, including three meals.

After you make your contribution it's time to sign up for a work team for the week. One of the unique characteristics about Taizé is that almost everyone works. The job options are plentiful, so if your first choice is taken you can always sign up for the bathroom cleaning crew (a job that isn't as bad as you might think!). Your options include the welcome team (the people who welcomed you signed up for that job prior to your arrival), cooking team, clean-up team, food distribution team, various cleaning teams, working in the Exposition (the gift shop) or Oyak (the snack shop), and several other jobs that must be filled in the community.

Once you've signed up for a work team you can stop by La Morada to deposit your passport and a few other valuables. Located directly across from Casa and adjacent to the kitchen, La Morada functions, in part, as a safety deposit box for valuables. Although Taizé is, for the most part, free of crime, the brothers encourage people to leave anything valuable in La Morada or

La Morada

to carry it with them at all times, since the dormitories are only locked during the prayers (when everyone is in the church). La Morada was first named "Tyniec" after a Benedictine monastery in Cracow, Poland. Brother Roger, however, felt that it was too difficult to pronounce, so they changed it to "The Yellow House." It was called the Yellow House for many years and, although it was an accurate description of the building, it seemed to "lack something." Thus, its name was eventually changed to La Morada, which means "the dwelling" in Spanish.

La Morada also functions a bit like a gateway to the brothers. If a visitor or group of people wants to meet with a brother, they must come to La Morada to make the appointment, and it's typically where the meeting will take place. Inside the waiting area is a large table with daily newspapers from various nations. In the colder months, a crackling fire burns from a hearth, offering considerable warmth. A larger room lies beyond the waiting area, with dividers and a dozen little partitioned nooks inside, each with a table, some chairs and, if you're lucky, a window looking out over the garden. In these rooms, the brothers meet with visitors to listen and to pray. Behind the building is a lovely garden, with a walk leading to the brothers' home and an old pottery studio where Brother Daniel, one of the first brothers, still works at his potter's wheel. Additionally, many of the young men who volunteer for longer periods at Taizé live next to La Morada. This location is ideal for the young men, because many of their duties are connected to welcoming people and assisting in the brothers' communication with the visitors.

SETTLING IN

Now that you've signed up for a work team and deposited your valuables at La Morada, you grab your backpack and head toward your accommodations for the night. Where you sleep in Taizé can vary quite a bit. If your lodging is in one of Taizé's signature blue tents or if you've brought your own tent, you cross west over the main road and walk down the hedge-lined path toward the camping fields. If you've brought your own tent, you're free to set up camp anywhere in the designated camping field, but if you're staying in one of the twenty-person blue tents, you must find your tent number and unpack your belongings there. The community uses the large blue tents primarily during the sum-mer months, but there are other times when they're set up to accommodate larger crowds.

If you're not camping for the week and were instead assigned to a bar-rack, which is similar to a dormitory, you make your way up the east side

The community's signature blue tents

Prayer shelter outside the church

of the road under the famous Taizé bells and into the meal area. On your right there is a large roof-covered area with terracotta-tiled floors. The washing-up signs and the eight large washbasins indicate that this is where the meals are distributed. To your left there is another roof-covered area with knee-high benches built into the ground and arranged in squares and triangles—enough seating for several hundred young people. As you continue forward, on your right you see a large tent suspended over a concrete slab with movable benches clustered in various seating arrangements. During the week, young people are packed like sardines in this area while meeting with their sharing groups after the Bible Introductions. On your left are enclosed meeting rooms, which are used for weekly workshops, various meetings, and the adult and family welcome. Directly in front of you as you move on is the Church of Reconciliation. Its east side is all that remains from the original church, which was completed in 1962. The brothers added the western extensions many years later to accommodate the growing number of pilgrims. Currently, the church holds about six thousand people. Much of the western exterior of the church has a wooden log veneer, giving it a rustic, yet still austere, appearance. Moving past the church toward the dormitories, you can't help but notice the Eastern Orthodox onion-shaped domes on top of the church and an outdoor chapel, which were added once Eastern Europeans were finally free to travel west.

Continuing forward on the path, you pass the Exposition, the small shop where the brothers sell their pottery, pendants, books, CDs and other merchandise—the only source of income for the brothers. With dinner rapidly approaching, however, you trudge on to find your dormitory. A small break in the hedge on your right reveals a small weathered picket fence with a rickety gate and a sign that reads "El Abiodh" (pronounced "el ah-bee-ohd"). A stone path leads up to a simple white building where, to the right of the doorway, another sign reads "El Abiodh." This building, whose name literally means "the white" in Arabic, was named not only for its color but more importantly after a place in the Sahara desert where a monastic community, the Little Brothers of Jesus, lives.[4]

El Abiodh was built in 1965 as Taizé's first guesthouse for the community. Up to that point in time, villagers welcomed the weary travelers into their homes. Today, the community continues to host pilgrims in El Abiodh's small rooms, although they reserve these accommodations for older visitors, the brothers' families and those with special needs. In addition to hosting guests, El Abiodh houses many of the long-term female permanents and several sisters from other orders who help in the community.[5] El Abiodh also contains a moderately sized kitchen, which is used to cook for the larger community during the busier times of the year (this is in addition to the industrial-sized kitchen, in which the meals for the larger crowds are prepared). Finally, the infirmary, which has its own exterior entrance, is also located in El Abiodh. Despite its limited hours, a nurse is usually available for most health-related issues you might encounter during your stay.

Shortly past El Abiodh, a large complex of guest rooms appears on your right. The brothers began building these dormitories in the early 1980s to accommodate the growing number of pilgrims. At one point the first dormitory, built in the early 1970s, needed to be torn

Dormitories

down to build new buildings that would hold more visitors. As you walk down the gravel and dirt road looking for your room number, young people flow in and out of their rooms. A barrage of laughter and different languages fills the air.

Once you find your room, you open the door to simple, yet quite functional accommodations. The floors are terra-cotta tile and, aside from the beds and one multishelved luggage rack, there is no furniture. Each room can hold up to eight or ten people on the metal bunk beds, which are equipped with a mattress and a clean fitted sheet. A single cable light hangs from the ceiling, shedding sparse but sufficient light. An ample window allows fresh air to circulate in the room during the day and night. With the capacity to offer accommodations for close to two thousand young people per week, the dormitories were a needed addition to the community. While tents are perfectly suitable for the late spring, summer and early autumn months, during those frigid winter months, the dormitories allow visitors to sleep in warm dry rooms.

With several bunks already spoken for, you decide to take one of the bottom bunks in the corner. You slide your backpack on the bottom shelf of the luggage rack and unfold your sleep sack. The soft bed feels tremendous after a long journey but, not wanting to fall asleep this late in the day, you decide to clean up before dinner. You quickly grab your towel and toiletries and make your way to the nearest bathroom, which is surprisingly clean considering the number of pilgrims staying at Taizé. Each shower stall contains a little bench for your belongings and a hook to hang your towel on, both in a partitioned section of the stall.

The actual shower experience at Taizé can be a little unpredictable. While a hot shower may be possible, if you shower at a high-traffic time, the light stream pouring from the shower head might be a bit on the chilly side. To make the event even more challenging, the water flow operates on a timed push-button mechanism, with each push affording you only about seven or eight seconds of water. By the second or third shower, though, most people get into the rhythm: scrub, push the button, scrub, push the button.

On your way out of the bathroom, you notice several cell phones plugged into the electrical outlets by the sinks. While at first this may seem odd, the explanation for it is quite reasonable. Electrical outlets at Taizé are few and far between. Other than the bathroom outlets, the only place to plug anything in is at random plugs located in the walkways of the dormitories. If you're lucky, your room will be adjacent to one. On one of my research trips, I was fortunate enough to have a plug just outside my window, which allowed me to charge my computer at night. On previous trips, however, I found myself using the little free time that I had to wait for it to charge.

DINNER IN TAIZÉ

After a shower and a change of clothing, you feel much better, and you quickly realize that it's drawing close to dinnertime, which is around 7:00 p.m. From most dormitories, it's about a five-minute walk to the eating area that you strolled by earlier. As you approach the food lines, you can see hundreds of young people already forming a massive disorganized queue leading up to the side of the distribution area. Imagine five-thousand-plus pilgrims swarming around like bees trying to enter their hive. Instead of a haunting buzz, though, an ocean of languages crashes around you, with the only universal language being laughter.

Taizé's famous red bowls

guage being laughter. Permanents shout from the front of the lines for extra help: "We need five people to help wash up. You get to eat first!" A few hungry souls move to the front of the line. Then the mass of young people breaks out in a Taizé chant to offer thanks. After two or three rounds, the crowd slowly starts to move.

Typical meal at Taizé

Little by little, you inch your body forward, uncertain of which line you will ultimately end up in. Aside from the vegetarian line on the far left, all the lines are the same. You finally find yourself in the front of the line and quickly hand your meal ticket to a young person who checks off the appropriate box. The next person on the distribution team hands you a scuffed brown tray, then a plate, a spoon and a bowl. Your utensils for the meal are complete. For North Americans this often comes as a surprise. No knife? What will I cut with? No fork? How will I pierce my food? No cup? How do you expect me to drink? No napkin? What if I get sauce on my face? Where am I?

Welcome to Taizé. At Taizé, simplicity is the golden rule. For the meals prepared there, a spoon is the only flatware you need. The bowl functions as a cup for tea or water (a custom that is still quite common for hot drinks in France today). As for the napkin—quite frankly, perhaps North Americans need to start eating more neatly. Then again, you could always use your bread to wipe your face.

Once you have all your utensils, you continue down the line. A young person on the distribution team scoops a hearty ladle of a rice and bean mixture onto your plate, while another places two slices of a baguette next to it. Another young person gives you a packaged cheese of some sort (often an herbed cream cheese spread, unless you're lucky enough to get a miniature wedge of the famous French Camembert), a piece of fruit, and a small package of cookies or cup of yogurt to finish off your meal. Occasionally, meat is part of the meal as well—a sausage link or chicken nugget, or perhaps even a slice of packaged ham. Once everyone has gone through the line, those with bigger appetites can return for seconds if there are leftovers.

On my first trip to Taizé, I packed protein energy bars and a few other nutrient-dense snacks for fear of there not being enough food. I have since relinquished that practice, in part to fully participate in the life of the community and in part to spiritually discipline myself to eat simply. I seriously doubt anyone would argue with the fact that, in North America, we have all sorts of food issues. From anorexia and obesity to the newest "beach" diet, North America has a distorted image of food. At Taizé, however, the food is simple and utilitarian. Don't get me wrong; it's filling and at times even tasty. But it's not meant to sustain you for your lifetime. It's not even meant to sustain you for several weeks at a time. It's designed to feed six thousand people in about an hour.

On one of my research trips, I ended up on the dinner work team. At five o'clock, I showed up at the back door of the kitchen and entered the changing area. Karin, the yearlong permanent from Austria who was in charge of making dinner, told me to take off my shoes and put on rubber clogs, an apron jacket and a disposable hat. With the other members of the cooking team, I received detailed instructions on proper hand-washing techniques, and only after we had all demonstrated that we understood her by actually washing our hands did we enter the kitchen. Nine industrial cooking pots lined the walls, several holding up to three hundred gallons of liquid

Making mashed potatoes

each. They were the largest cooking pots I had ever seen; you could comfortably fit two humans in some of them! We proceeded to dump crate after crate of fusilli pasta into the huge cauldrons filled with boiling water. In the other pots, we made a very basic tomato sauce out of canned tomatoes and various herbs and spices. After the pasta was ready, we drained the water, added the sauce and mixed them together. Once thoroughly mixed, we scooped the pasta into large aluminum serving containers, placed these containers in insulated boxes and stacked them by the door for the food transportation team to take them to the distribution area.

After cleaning up, we ate together in a small eating area off the changing room. Most meals at Taizé are easy to prepare and serve, and each step of the process has a different team of young people assigned to take care of it. From preparing the food for cooking, actually doing the cooking and transporting the food to the distribution area to serving, collecting dishes and washing up the dishes, the young people are completely responsible for every step. At Taizé, the young people serve each other.

The Church of Reconciliation

After your meal you drop your dishes off with the washing-up team and then make your way toward the Church of Reconciliation. Though it's a little early for evening prayers, young people are already outside the doors of

Washing basins in the kitchen

the church holding up long rectangular signs with the word *Silence* on them in various languages. You enter and pick up a Taizé songbook, the reading for the prayer time and the supplemental song sheet. The lighting is dim and the faint smell of incense lingers. There are already many young seekers scattered across the church. Most are seated on the floor, but there are a few people sitting on wooden benches that line the walls of the church. You make your way down the makeshift aisles, demarcated by long strips of masking tape, and find a spot on the ground a short distance from a row of short, artificial hedges that separate the brothers from the rest of pilgrims. The ground is hard, even though it's covered in a commercial carpet. The rough, plastic fibers are smashed down, giving the carpet an almost smooth texture. On the warmest days in Taizé, the church can smell a little like feet, which is part of the reason that the brothers have the permanents walk the incense burners up and down the aisles. Nothing destroys the spirit of prayer like the subtle smell of feet!

After settling in, you gaze around the church with wonder. The Church of Reconciliation is not like a traditional European church. The whole building has a slight decline eastward toward the front of the church. It doesn't really have a nave (the long part where the congregation sits), nor does it have transepts (the "wings" that extend out from the nave, giving many churches the shape of a cross). It does have a chancel of sorts (the area that separates the nave from the high altar), however, the brothers simply call this front area "the choir." Historically, the choir was the area between the nave and the chancel where the choir would sing. Although there is no embodied choir in Taizé, the brothers have continued to call the whole area "the choir."

The most notable features of the choir area are candle-filled chimney blocks and signature orange sails. Both have surprisingly unique twists in their design. First, imagine dozens of square, hollow, terra-cotta chimney blocks stacked on their sides so that you can see through their hollowed middles. In the hollow of each block a single candle sits. The famous Taizé blocks found their way into the church's choir by accident. In the mid 1970s an old altar was removed from the church, so the brothers stacked some chimney blocks left over from a building project in its place. Stacking the blocks in the shape of an altar and placing candles in them created a simple yet beautiful focal point. Additionally, they hung a two-meter band of orange material behind the blocks to reflect the light.

The flickering glow in the blocks reminded Brother Roger of the ancient Christian catacombs in Rome. As history tells us, Christians used to light candles, place them in the narrow niches where the bodies where buried and offer prayers in memory of those who died. For some in Taizé this block altar became a kind of symbol that linked the prayers of the brothers with the Christians who preceded them. When the brothers determined that the blocks contributed to an atmosphere of prayer, they decided to order several dozen more and fill the choir area with them. Since that time, they have rearranged the blocks in different formations and replaced the terra-cotta altar with a more traditional one. Despite these changes, the blocks remain a long-standing part of the church's décor.

When the original altar was removed from the church, a large candelabrum that hung in the center of the choir was also removed. Consequently, for many years the vaulted ceiling was void of any significant focal point. In an attempt to fill this space in the mid 1980s, one of the brothers designed long strips of orange and red fabric that hung from the ceiling. These bands looked as if they were linking heaven and earth, and like the chimney blocks, the brothers saw them as both simple and beautiful. For many years the banners filled the open space of the choir.

The reason why the banners were cut into sails is a testimony to both the creativity and practicality of the brothers. As the European meetings became more prominent (the European meetings are gatherings in which the brothers meet with tens of thousands of young people in other European cities to pray), the brothers decided to take their banners with them. Many of the exposition halls in which the meetings took

Inside the church

place charged the brothers for every point from which each banner was hung. One point for each banner was far less expensive that two points; consequently, the brothers cut several of the banners into triangles so they could hang each banner from one point—and the well-known Taizé sails were born. Though not all present-day sails are triangles, the brothers kept the shape, as it offered yet another symbol. While the long rectangle banners seemed to connect heaven and earth, the sails evoked symbolic images of the flames of the Holy Spirit and boat sails. One of the brothers fully embraces the latter imagery, commenting that the sails offer us a reminder that the church progresses forward not by our rowing but by the breath of the Holy Spirit.

In addition to the sails and the lit chimney blocks, there are also several icons on display in the choir. Icons first appeared in Taizé around the 1950s and have remained ever since. Despite the fact that Brother Roger was from a Swiss Reformed Protestant tradition, where icons would have never been utilized, his exposure to their sacramental function in Christianity stemmed back to his childhood. When he was three years old, living in Switzerland, his parents occasionally offered lodging to Russian refugees. These refugees had very few possessions, but their meager earthly belongings often included Christian icons. Consequently, he was exposed to various icons from the Orthodox tradition at a very early age. In the 1950s, Brother Roger incorporated icons into the prayers because he thought they might be helpful aids in worship. Among the notable icons in the church today, you can find one of the Virgin Mary holding the Christ child, which was painted by Brother Eric, who died in the autumn of 2007. He is also responsible for painting the Cross of Taizé, which stands on the right side of the choir area. This cross has become a significant icon in the community both in the brothers' own prayers and in the European meetings (as it travels with them).

A short, one-foot hedge in the shape of a rectangle separates the area where the brothers pray from the rest of the assembly. It begins at the steps of the altar and ends about a third of the way into the church. While the current hedges have only been up since the early 1990s, there has always been a subtle distinction between the brothers and the visitors since the time when the brothers originally prayed in the old village church. This distinction is not meant to divide *them* from *us,* but rather to allow the brothers to maintain a sense of identity as a community. As part of their vows, they commit to pray together three times a day. In this regard, it is essential for them to reserve space to fulfill that covenant. It's also important for the larger gathering of pilgrims to see the brothers praying together, as their unified presence at the center of the church offers an important symbol of their life together.

Without a doubt, Taizé is filled with symbolism. In fact, over the years differing accounts have been purported as to what the various symbols mean. Note, however, that at Taizé, there is no unifying or single symbolic imagery that the brothers are attempting to employ. Each brother will find different meanings in the symbols around the church, and likewise, each pilgrim is free to interpret these symbols in their own way. This is an important aspect of Taizé. The brothers purposely use symbols with open meanings. One of the brothers explained that symbols should never be closed: "Symbols are meant to be suggestive, not prescriptive." Thus, most of the décor and sacred art in the church is left open for the pilgrim to interpret. In this way, "the Spirit can speak to us deep within our hearts."

At the front of the church is an elevated pipe organ about twelve feet off the ground and a door underneath it through which the brothers can access it. A table with an icon of the Virgin Mary on it sits just to the right of the organ. Mounted on the wall above the table is a sacristy that holds the Roman Catholic reserve sacrament—consecrated Eucharistic elements that remain after a service.

On the far right side of the choir area there is a wooden partition that covers the doorway through which the brothers enter the church. Various soft orange light fixtures and artificial greenery are attached to it, creating a sublime setting for another important aspect of the sanctuary—but one with a rather dubious reputation. Just to the right of the partition is a curtain that many English-speaking pilgrims have referred to as the "Oz curtain," because they're unaware of what lies behind it. Casting off any notions of sacrilege, I'm happy to report that there is no man behind the curtain; rather the Protestant Communion elements are placed there after they are consecrated in an early-morning service.

On the right side of the church, Brother Eric installed a series of stained-glass windows, recessed into the wall. Each window bears a different biblical motif in vivid color. Because of their subtle location, however, many pilgrims don't have the opportunity to experience them. In addition to these windows, two other places in the church hold stained glass. On the borders of the ceiling, long panels of orange and blue stained glass offer the church a little extra light. These functional yet beautiful additions were constructed by Brother Denis, the architect of the church. Pilgrims often remark that the upper windows give the church a Noah's ark feel.

Additionally, when the church was built in 1962, another brother, Brother Marc, created a large stained-glass window for the west wall and two long vertical windows for the choir. The western window offered warming beams of light during the evening prayers, but in 1971 the west wall was torn down to accommodate more pilgrims. Thus, the only remnants of his work that remain are the two vertical pieces running the length of the church wall on each side of the choir. It's bittersweet that only a fraction of Brother Marc's stained-glass mastery still remains—a small memory of the community's incredible journey.

EVENING PRAYERS

One by one the brothers begin to file into the church. Cloaked in all-white prayer habits, they take their seats within the hedge-bordered area at the center of the church. Some brothers sit on the ground, others use prayer benches, and a few sit on basic wooden chairs next to the hedge line. The contrast between the white of their robes and the orange décor is a striking sight.

You might be wondering why there's so much orange in Taizé. When I first visited the community I asked that same question. One person told me that the brothers borrowed it from the Asian monastic tradition while an-

The bell tower

other person said they use it because it's the color of fire, which represents the Holy Spirit. When I asked one of the brothers, he explained, "Orange is both warm and bright. Yellow doesn't have the warmth, and red doesn't have the light. It suggests warmth. It's not quite fire, but it's . . . amber burning, giving heat." None of these responses really satisfied my curiosity, however. When I eventually did find out the real reason for the prominence of orange at Taizé, all I could do was smile: one of the brothers admitted quite frankly, "It was Brother Roger's favorite color."

As more people filter in, the sounds of the campus bells resound through the church. The Taizé bells, which are located between Casa and the food distribution area, can be heard throughout the grounds of the community and village. Those who have visited Taizé know the sound of the bell's disordered yet strangely melodic gonging. The bells ring three times a day to summon everyone on campus to come to the church. For many young people, it becomes not just a signal that prayers will begin in about eight minutes, but it also functions as a call to worship and an invitation to settle their spirits before God.

The church is now crowded and, with very little space around you, you realize you have become one pilgrim in a sea of spiritual seekers. While there are always a few people squirming around when the bells stop, for the most part, the church is quiet. One of the brothers opens with the refrain of a song and the rest of the assembly joins in. The song numbers are illuminated through little red LED number displays (the kind that some churches use for nursery paging) that are carefully positioned around the church. There are no overheads, video projectors or PowerPoint presentations at Taizé; only these unobtrusive electronic displays and six thousand songbooks.

After a few chants, everyone turns to the lectern and one of the brothers reads a passage of Scripture. Then, after a response, an extended period of silence begins. Outside of the occasional cough or sneeze, the church is utterly still for the whole period, which can last anywhere between eight to twelve minutes. The brothers like to say that when young people first come to Taizé, the time of silence is too long, but by the time they leave, it's too short. When the silence is broken, intercessions are offered in different languages with the community singing one variety of "Kyrie Eleison" as a response. After a few more songs, the prior of the community (now Brother Alois), who sits the farthest away from the altar table, stands up and walks down through the seated brothers and exits the building. As he leaves most of the brothers join him, although a few remain to continue praying. A few minutes later Brother Alois returns with some of the brothers and they situate themselves around the church so they're available to listen to the young pilgrims.

AFTER THE PRAYERS

Though the prayer time has officially ended, many of the young people will remain to pray into the evening. Those who decide not to stay gather their belongings and exit the church. Exhaustion sets in again for you, so you head back to your dormitory to go to bed early. As you walk to the back of the church, you take one final look: the remaining pilgrims pepper the floor softly singing one of the chants. You return your songbook and papers and exit the building. As you emerge from the church, the dampness of the night air catches you off-guard. It's surprisingly refreshing, almost invigorating. Pockets of young people converse as they make their way toward the village. At first you wonder where everyone is headed, but you quickly remember that after eve-

Oyak

ning prayers, Oyak opens. Oyak, which is across the road from Casa, is the only designated "hang out" area at Taizé. Getting a second wind, you decide to check it out.

You know as you cross the road and walk down the western hedge-lined path that you're drawing near, because you can hear the soft hum of people talking growing louder with each step you take. When you turn the corner at the end of the hedge, only a parking lot separates you from Oyak. It's a rectangular building with an expansive awning that stretches around two sides of the building, offering sufficient cover in times of inclement weather. Numerous lampposts illuminate the area, providing just enough light for visitors to socialize around high tables and a few clusters of wooden benches. Everyone is crammed around the tables, drinking sodas, cider, beer, wine, coffee and hot chocolate. Some are eating purchased food while others smoke cigarettes. As you make your way past the wire-bound picket fence to the end of the queue, laughter mixed with other languages (French, German, Spanish, Polish, Italian and many others that you can't recognize) fills the air, all blending together in a cacophony of sound—chaos meets beauty.

Taizé's Oyak was named after a town in Cameroon near the large port city of Douala (which happens to also be the name of the area where young people can pitch their tents). It opened in the early 1980s; before its construction, there wasn't an official gathering place for young people at Taizé. Pilgrims would instead congregate around the meal distribution area, their tents and the dormitories.

Centralizing the pilgrims' evening socializing, however, was not the original impetus behind Oyak's establishment. With the steady influx of visitors to Taizé, the brothers knew that it wouldn't be long before outside vendors would prey upon the young people. Visions of hot-dog trucks parked on the side of the road outside the church, peddling food and drinks, concerned the brothers enough to consider building their own concession area. While someone driving a hot-dog truck (or the like) could still attempt to make a profit on Taizé's transient population, chances are they would fail. The brothers, in fact, have almost guaranteed that no vendors will ever capitalize on the grumbling bellies of the visitors by selling everything at Oyak at the lowest possible price. Not a single cent is collected beyond what it takes to keep Oyak's doors open.

Oyak also houses a little shop called the Bazaar. The Bazaar also sells all its wares at their actual cost value. For example, a bar of chocolate is one-fifth what it would be in a store outside the community. In addition to chocolate and other snacks (both savory and sweet), you can purchase extra toiletries (shampoo, toothpaste, tissues, feminine products, etc.), batteries and large bottles of water. When the Bazaar is closed, smaller bottles of water may be purchased at the vending machines on the south side of the building.

Beer and wine are also sold at a fraction of what it would cost at a local restaurant. Like most of Europe, the legal drinking age in France is lower than in the United States. Eighteen-year-olds are able to purchase alcohol in Taizé; however, there is a fairly strict one-drink maximum for all ages. For those under eighteen who are craving a malty beverage on a hot summer's day, nonalcoholic beer or cider may be purchased through the exterior window of Oyak. Those seeking regular beers and wines have to enter the actual building. Although it is permissible to drink in Taizé, Oyak is the only place on the campus where a visitor can consume alcohol. In fact, if you purchase bottles of the famous French Burgundy wine before entering the community, the brothers ask you to leave them at La Morada. Upon your departure, you can retrieve your wine and any other items you might have checked.

With a cup of coffee and a bar of dark French chocolate in hand, you make your way out of Oyak and follow the sounds of music to the south side

Oyak at night

of the building. Under a huge tent, hoards of young people have gathered in a large circle. Several are playing guitars and many in the lively crowd are dancing and singing along. The dancing, laughing and merry-making in general will continue into the night. You, on the other hand, have reached your limit. After watching the energetic mass for a little longer, you head back to your dormitory. Before calling it a night, you decide to make a quick phone call to let your loved ones back home know that you've arrived safely.

There are public phones in two locations in Taizé. The first is directly across from Casa, by the road next to Oyak. The second place is midway between the Exposition and the dormitories on the west side of the road. There are a dozen phones at each location where international phone cards may be used. Nearby the second cluster of phones sits a little Internet hut. Although it's pricey, a visitor can access their email or surf the Web at this location using their credit card. After letting your loved ones know that you're safe and sound, you finally make it back to your bed. The minute your head hits your pillow, you're . . . zzzzzzzzz (out for the night).

3

Exploring the Community

Tu sei sorgente viva, tu sei fuoco, sei carità.
(You are the living source ; you are fire and love.)
Vieni Spirito Santo, vieni Spirito Santo.
(Come Holy Spirit, come Holy Spirit.)

The morning clatter in the dormitories made it completely unnecessary to set your alarm, although you remain in bed until the incessant beeping of your clock motivates you to get up and turn it off. You look at the time and realize that you only have twenty minutes to make it to morning prayers. Quickly jumping out of bed, you make your way to the bathrooms to join the long row of bleary-eyed teeth brushers. With a splash of water on your face and a change of clothing, you're on your way to the Church of Reconciliation. En route to the church, the bells begin to gong, which quickens everyone's pace. With the hundreds of other young people, you squeeze through the church doors, grab your prayer book and find any available space still left on the floor. From the flood of sniffles, morning coughs and throat clearing filling the atmosphere, it's clear that many young people have just rolled out

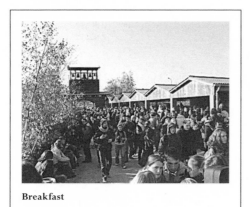

Breakfast

of bed; nevertheless, as the bells come to a halt, so also do the bodily groans of six thousand tired pilgrims.

With the exception of the Eucharist in the morning prayers, the flow of the liturgy is very similar to the prayers of the previous evening. One striking difference is that very few people linger after the brothers leave the church. No doubt this is because breakfast is distributed immediately following the morning prayers. Just like the dinner queues the night before, you join the herd of young people pooling toward the food lines. After a sung prayer for the meal, the crowd quickly presses forward. The line for breakfast moves more rapidly than other meals, because at Taizé, breakfast is especially simple. In fact, they don't even use meal tickets during breakfast. You find out why as you approach the distribution team: you're handed a little baguette (five or six inches long), a pat of foil-wrapped butter and a piece of dark chocolate the size of a stick of chewing gum. They also hand you a bowl, which you can choose to fill with hot chocolate or hot tea (of course, you can also opt for water as well). Many visitors use the piece of chocolate as a butter knife, which works well so long as you are there during the warmer months of the year when the butter is soft. (When I was in Taizé one cold November, I literally broke my chocolate knife in the pat of butter, so I ended up eating the butter like a cookie . . . mmmm.) Once everyone is through the line, some people go back for an extra baguette, and during the less busy times of the year there might even be some leftover fruit from the previous day's meals.

As you finish your last bite of the baguette, you drop your bowl off in a big blue bucket for the clean-up team and head over to Oyak for coffee. (Yes, I know you've just had hot chocolate, but when I'm in Taizé, a second hot drink—one that contains caffeine—has become part of my morning ritual. So that's where you're headed!) A dozen or so smokers sit on the benches at Oyak, having their morning fix of nicotine and caffeine. Although the concession windows and the Bazaar are only open during certain hours of the day, the instant coffee machine on the north side of the building is available all day long. Coffee, tea, hot chocolate and an instant soup mix are available through the machine. Don't be fooled though; the hot beverages that this machine produces are not of the high standard you'd find in a French coffee shop. There is no little barista inside the machine frothing your milk with an espresso machine. The drinks are, however, hot and quickly become a welcomed part of many of the pilgrims' daily routine.

BIBLE INTRODUCTIONS

After finishing your drink, you head toward the Church of Reconciliation. From Monday through Saturday each week, most visitors spend their late mornings in a biblical teaching time the brothers call Bible Introductions.

During the busier months, there are two or three options from which to choose, but during the less crowded times, most pilgrims are divided into groups by language only. Typically, a brother will meet with a few volunteer leaders before the start of the Introduction. These young people will lead the small discussion groups for the remainder of the week. He gives them a paper with questions for that day and shares with them the most salient points of the passage.

A Bible Introduction

A sharing group

As pilgrims enter the church, which is now partitioned by pull-down metal dividers, they go to the area where the different Introductions will be presented. There are often pockets of different languages in each Bible Introduction, with a person from each group acting as the translator. In a Bible Introduction during the summer, you could have up to four or five languages being spoken at any given point.

On Monday, the brother will introduce the book or topic for the week and then proceed to read the text, often in several languages. For example, he might read it first in English and then in German. If other language groups are present, he would then allow for the individual translators to read the passage to that group. Once the text is read, the brother offers an expository lesson on the passage. Going through a text or narrative verse by verse provides enough time and space for each language group to discover the events or message of the section of Scripture. Presenting the Bible Introductions in this manner, however, sometimes has a disjointed effect, as each language group must wait for other translations to take place. When the actual teaching time ends (which usually takes between thirty minutes and an hour, depending on the number of translations needed for the session), sharing groups begin.

On the first day, the brothers invite you to cluster into small groups according to language. Not everyone in your sharing group may speak your native language fluently, though it may be the most comprehensible language available that week. For example, during one visit, I had three Germans and four Swedes in my sharing group, and amazingly, English was the common language. We muddled through the texts and questions with a fair amount of laughter, and when everyone was thoroughly exhausted, we'd head to Oyak for coffee. (If you haven't gathered by now, I love the instant coffee machine.)

The sharing groups become an important part of understanding the communal life at Taizé. Not only does it offer a chance to work through a passage of Scripture, it affords you a chance to experience the text from another cultural perspective. In the sharing groups, the horizons of each individual fuse and you begin to see that, despite our differences, humans across the globe struggle with the same issues. You begin to realize that you are not alone in your spiritual journey, but rather you have joined a company of sojourners in a pilgrimage of trust on earth. Without question, the Bible Introductions and sharing groups are among the most significant moments you can experience in Taizé.

After you're done with your Bible Introduction and sharing group, there is a short break before the midday prayers. As people enter the church shortly after noon, there is a mixed feeling in the air. For some, midday prayer is the most difficult of the three, whereas for others, a joyful energy ensues. The tired disposition of many young people appears only more pronounced by the jubilant nature of others. You find a spot on the floor and settle in. Of all three prayers, the midday prayers are the shortest, lasting around thirty minutes. Again, like the morning prayers, very few people linger for contemplation after the brothers leave, since lunch immediately follows.

AFTERNOONS IN TAIZÉ

Like the other meals, the lines at lunch are chaotic. The distribution line is similar to the dinner meal: tray, plate, bowl, spoon, a scoop of something, bread, cheese, fruit and cookies. Different distribution and clean-up teams work during lunch and dinner, so once their assigned meal is over, they've contributed their work time to the life of the pilgrim community for the day.

Since at Taizé almost everyone works, the afternoon is usually designated for work teams whose jobs aren't time specific. There are a few work teams that clean during the morning sharing groups in exchange for meeting with their

Sweeping in front of the church

groups in the afternoon, but for many, the afternoons are spent working.

You make your way to your job for the week: cleaning the area around the church. With a broom in one hand and a trash bag in the other, you and ten other pilgrims begin sweeping the pavement in front of the church. Although most visitors to Taizé don't litter, a fair amount of trash still finds its way under the bushes and in various corners of the grounds. It is quite common to see work teams singing and smiling; in fact, outside of the prayers many young people find that the communal work is one of their favorite parts of their stay in Taizé. This is partly due to the sense of community that is formed in the work groups. After a couple of hours, you and your team are done, and the area around the church is once again litter free.

With nothing but optional workshops late in the afternoon, you're finally free to participate in a variety of different activities. Although the brothers prefer everyone to remain on the grounds, there is inevitably always a group of people going into Cluny for some sightseeing. For those who do remain on the grounds, there are many different ways to spend the free time. People often walk around the old village of Taizé and visit the small church that the first brothers used for prayers. It's a quaint little Romanesque church with several beautiful stained-glass windows, which are only noticeable from the center of the church. In front and to the right of the church lies a small cemetery where a few brothers, including Brother Roger, are buried. During the afternoon, some people simply hang out at Oyak and have a beer and some chips. Others may choose to take a walk to Saint Steven's Source *(La Source de Saint Etienne),* a wooded area filled with winding paths that lead down to a lake complete with a bubbling brook, a small waterfall and a charming little bridge over the water. Although the hours for the Source are limited, it's a treasure at Taizé that many visitors overlook.

A path in Saint Steven's Source

Some pilgrims make their way to the Exposition to peruse the brothers' pottery and other assorted items that are available for purchase. Wanting to take a look at the pottery yourself, you wander through the doors of the Exposition. Inside, the lighting is warm and inviting. In one corner of the room, dozens of books arranged by language are available, while another corner is filled with various postcards featuring pictures of the community, the brothers' artwork and a potpourri of other designs. On plexiglass-encased pedestals, enameled pendants are on display. In addition to the famous Taizé dove-cross pendants, the brothers also make circular and leaf-shaped pendants that are associated with particular passages in Scripture.

Although the Taizé dove-cross symbol was created around 1970, it wasn't until the early 1980s that the brothers considered it a symbol of the community. Their rationale for the production of the pendants was twofold. First, the dove-cross pendant offered a way for young people to remember the transformation they felt during their time in the community. It allowed them to take with them a tangible reminder of the peace and reconciliation they experienced while in Taizé. The symbol contains both the dove— a universal sign for peace—and the cross, which from a Judeo-Christian perspective embodies the reconciliation that we received through Christ's death. Second, because the pendant looks a bit more like a dove than a cross, many Eastern Europeans could wear the Christian cross in countries that forbade anyone to wear one. If asked what was around their neck, they could simply reply, "A dove."

Dove-cross pendant

Unlike the dove-cross pendants, pottery has been a part of the community since the late 1940s as a way for the brothers to earn their living, though the current Exposition was built only twenty years ago. From simple bowls and plates to large vases and Communion sets, the brothers make hundreds of pieces a week. In addition to these items, the brothers also sell CDs and DVDs about the community, sheet music, icons in various sizes, posters of the stained-glass windows, and prayer stools. The sale of each of these items supports the common life of the brothers; in fact, it is their only income, as the brothers do not take contributions or donations for their own livelihood.

With a mental list of items to buy later in the week, you decide to only purchase a pendant. As you walk back to your dormitory to freshen up before dinner, your body begins experiencing the pangs of exhaustion again. Once in the room, you surrender to your tiredness and lay down to rest until dinner, which is less than two hours away.

That's pretty much it: your first twenty-four hours in Taizé. Granted, you probably wouldn't see that much in the first twenty-four hours, but the rhythm of life is true to the description. With the exception of a few meetings and two specific alterations in the Friday and Saturday evening prayers, the schedule at Taizé doesn't really change. This simple schedule helps visitors quickly acclimate to life in the community. Usually by Tuesday or, at the latest, Wednesday, pilgrims young and old find their way easily in the community. By the end of the week, many say it feels like home, at least in the spiritual sense. In fact, for almost six decades, visitors have called Taizé their spiritual home. Thus, each time they return, it's like a homecoming. Why? Much of the mystery of and attraction to this unique community stems from the life of Brother Roger, who through a commitment to his own spiritual convictions created a life and guided a community that ushers in reconciliation to a world in desperate need of peace.

4

Brother Roger and the Formation of a Community

Ubi caritas et amor, ubi caritas Deus ibi est.
(Where there is charity and love, God is to be found.)

When people hear the word *Taizé,* they often associate it with a style of music or with specific songs like "Ubi Caritas" and "Bless the Lord." Some may have heard of Brother Roger or know that Taizé is a place in France, while others associate Taizé with a monastic tradition of chants and contemplative spirituality. While all these associations have an authentic reflection of truth in them, they are only glimmers of the actual community of Taizé.

Despite what some may assume, unlike many monastic communities, Taizé doesn't have a long history. In fact, at the time of this writing the community is only sixty-seven years old. It was on August 20, 1940, that a young man named Roger rode his bike from a nearby town and discovered a desolate little village in the Burgundy region of southern France. That village was Taizé.

From his first arrival in the village of Taizé to the final evening of his death, Brother Roger's life tells the story of a relentless pursuit of a lived gospel. The Taizé community has a unique history that spans just under seven decades, and while this isn't a long period, the development of this ecumenical community of brothers is filled with amazing stories that reveal the earnest quest of one man who sought to make his life a living example of the gospel. Several important threads woven into the history of this community make its story worth telling. Brother Roger and the ordinary yet committed brothers who joined him were characterized by intentionality, determination and adaptability. Through their life together, they have aimed at unapologetically incarnating the gospel; their story is marked by their care for the poor and love for their neighbor. Focusing on the gospel's essence has enabled them to speak into the lives of millions of young people over the years.

It is in these endeavors and priorities that their desire and longing for reconciliation and peace can be undoubtedly seen. In fact, as they have grown, the theme that continues to emerge is their call for reconciliation—with God, with others and with ourselves. Moreover, through their quest for reconciliation we are privileged to witness one of their most inspiring and admirable qualities in action: adaptability. In their development as a community, they have consistently listened and adapted to the call of God upon their collective life. They've never embodied a "build it and they will come" mentality, but rather time and again they have faced the questions, "What do we do now?" "How do we faithfully care for those whom God has put on our path?" They asked themselves, again and again, "How do we live out the gospel in and through our lives?" What follows in this chapter is the story of the Taizé community.[1]

THE EARLY YEARS OF ROGER LOUIS SCHUTZ-MARSAUCHE: 1915-1942

On May 12, 1915, in the village of Provence, Switzerland, a baby boy was born to his French mother, Amélie Marsauche, and his Swiss father, Charles Schutz. His seven sisters (he was the youngest of nine children) chose the name *Roger* for the new baby.[2] Brother Roger's father was a Swiss Protestant pastor in the Reformed tradition; his mother was also a Protestant and was from a French family whose roots trace back to the Burgundy region of France. Although raised in Switzerland, young Roger always had an affinity for France—no doubt to the credit of his mother.

At a young age, Brother Roger also developed a love for music through influences on both sides of his family. His mother, Amélie, grew up in a very musical family and, as a consequence, studied singing in Paris prior to her arranged marriage to Charles Schutz, who expressed his musical proclivity through the violin (albeit reportedly not very well).[3] Knowing this, it's easy to see why the Taizé prayers center on a sung liturgy.

In addition to their love for music, Brother Roger's parents also shared a love for the poor. As the story goes, when he was thirteen, Roger needed to attend secondary school in another village. His father was faced with two boarding options for Roger: a Protestant family or a poor, Roman Catholic widow with several children. The Swiss pastor eventually chose the Catholic widow because she needed the money more.

Living with his landlady, Madame Bioley, was not Roger's first experience with Catholicism. He recalled stories from his childhood when his grandmother not only attended the Catholic Mass but also received the Catholic Eucharist. He also remembered as a twelve-year-old seeing his father enter Catholic churches to pray—a rather unusual practice for Reformed clergy, even today. During the years he lived with Madame Bioley, though, young Roger did struggle with his faith. The dissension between Protestants and Catholics forced him to question his own beliefs. Yet, living in the tension of his own Protestantism and Madame Bioley's Roman Catholicism may also have helped shape Brother Roger's deep longing for reconciliation. No one at that time could have ever guessed that years later, he would eventually lead one of the most significant ecumenical movements of our era.

In 1931, when he was sixteen, Roger contracted tuberculosis, quite possibly from Madame Bioley's youngest daughter.[4] Although he became very sick, even to the point of death, Roger managed to slowly recover. This period of recovery was marked by his own studies and long periods of isolation in the Swiss mountain air. Spending time alone increased his appreciation for silence and contemplation—significant aspects of the Taizé prayers today. Once fully recovered, Brother Roger began to consider what career he would pursue.

Despite the fact that his father wanted him to study theology, Roger decided that he would pursue a literary career and become a writer and a farmer. During his years in recovery from tuberculosis, he wrote a short novel titled *Evolution of a Puritan Boyhood*. It was accepted for publication in the nationally respected *Nouvelle Revue Française (The New French Review),* provided that he make several changes to the end. Roger, however, felt he couldn't conscientiously comply with the publisher's request, as the changes would have made his final assertions untrue. Interpreting this experience as a sign that his near-budding literary career was never meant to be, he succumbed to the wishes of his father and enrolled to study theology in 1936, which he did for the next four years at the Universities of Lausanne and Strasbourg.

After his first year of theological studies in Lausanne, Roger began to doubt his decision. The summer of 1937 proved to be a significant time for the young, confused theologian. His sister, Lily, became very ill during her pregnancy, and death seemed inevitable. For the first time, Roger really cried out to God. Through the simple phrase from the Psalms, "It is your face that I seek, O Lord," Roger looked to God to intervene. When Lily pulled through, he took it as an indication to register for his second year of theological studies. For the next two years, he continued his studies in Lausanne, and partly in Strasbourg.

In 1939, on the eve of his final year, a group of classmates approached Roger with a strange request: they wanted him to become the next president of the Student Christian Association. It was a surprising offer considering he had only been to one meeting (which he didn't like) and hadn't spent much time with the members of the group. Despite his initial refusal, Roger eventually conceded to their offer and took on the leadership of the association, a decision that would prove far more formative than he could have imagined. That winter, Roger devised a series of Bible studies that focused on the foundations of faith and prayer as a means to search for God.[5] Slowly the association grew, and before long they were meeting in a large auditorium at the University of Lausanne.

As this student group expanded, a smaller group emerged out of it. Under Roger's leadership, twenty students formed an intentional community called La Grande Communauté. The community became a kind of "third order" which met every other month for retreats and discussion.[6] These retreats were characterized by an authentic search for God through prayer, silence, meditation and confession. Eventually, Roger's involvement and leadership in La Grande Communauté affected his studies. So distracted by his thoughts on community and a Christ-centered life, Roger was unable to finish a short thesis—his last requirement for graduation. Furthermore, his plans for the future were uncertain, as the war had begun during his final year of study, and already a large part of France was under a German regime.

Germany's control of France was difficult for Roger, as he still had many relatives on his mother's side living there. During the winter of his final year of studies, Roger spent many days praying about La Grande Communauté's role in the growing conflict. They had dreamed about a house in which they would live as a community of reconciliation, but Roger didn't know exactly how it would come to fruition. Years later he wrote, "The defeat of France awoke powerful sympathy. If a house could be found there, of the kind we had dreamed of, it would offer a possible way of assisting some of those most discouraged, those deprived of a livelihood; and it could become a place of silence and work."[7]

This powerful sympathy eventually moved Roger to pursue his dream of a house in France. He asked a few of his closest friends from the university to join him, but they declined his offer. While disappointed, their disinterest couldn't deter Roger from responding to this call, so he set out alone in his quest for a house.

On only his bicycle Roger traveled to the Burgundy region of France, which was one of the unoccupied areas under the control of Marshal Pétain and the Vichy government. War refugees—many of whom were Jews—were fleeing to the free areas of France like Burgundy. Roger had several areas in the region in mind as possibilities. The first house he found was too close to the busyness of the Lyon-Geneva railway; the noise alone would have been problematic. He discovered a second house, which seemed almost perfect, except for its proximity to Geneva; it was too close to home. A third house was located in Bourg-en-Bresse. Roger felt it was too comfortable, though, and feared it would not encourage creativity, so he continued on in his search. While passing through Mâcon he realized that the ancient Cluny Abbey was nearby and felt that he had to stop and visit the site.

The Cluny Abbey was founded on September 2, 909, by William I, the count of Auvergne. A Benedictine order established itself in the Cluny monastery and eventually, through its influence, transformed Cluny into one of the most significant cities in Europe. In fact, up to the sixteenth century, Cluny boasted the largest ecclesial edifice in Europe before the Vatican renovated St. Peter's Cathedral in Rome. In 1790, however, the city was attacked and destroyed during the French Revolution and only fragments of the once great Cluny Cathedral remain. The church was never reconstructed because the residents used the rubble from the former church to rebuild their own homes. Although Cluny is now known for its significance in the development of Western monasticism, it's become more of a tourist attraction than a holy destination. It's perhaps ironic in that sense that Brother Roger found the desolate village of Taizé only a few kilometers from the once great Cluny.

Cluny

Once in Cluny, Brother Roger inquired about properties for sale in the area. A local lawyer pointed him to a sizable house in a small village called Taizé. Late in the morning on August 20, 1940, Brother Roger rode his bike to the little village. Upon his arrival, he was struck by how bleak the village appeared—it lacked paved roads and many of the houses were empty. The family who owned the house for sale lived in Lyon, but an old woman who lived in the village was available to show the property to Brother Roger. Although much of the land surrounding the property had already been sold, the house and the buildings adjacent to it, which appeared to be in good condition, were still available for purchase. Brother Roger is often remembered as saying that the sale price wasn't more than the price of two cars, making it a viable option.

It was late in the day when they finished looking at the property, so the woman invited Brother Roger to stay for a meal. While they were eating, Brother Roger explained his dream for the future. The woman pleaded with him to remain in the village: "Buy the house and stay here . . . we are all alone." The desperate appeal of the poor woman moved Roger. In his spirit, he knew that Christ speaks through the poor; consequently, he decided to purchase the house. Less than a month later, Roger signed the deed to the house, and plans were already underway for the first gathering of La Grande Communauté. It was December 1940 before the community had its first official meeting, but Roger had already been living in the house in attempts to minister to the poor.[8]

Taizé was only a few miles from the demarcation line separating the German-occupied region of France from free territory under the control of the Vichy regime. Through covert connections in Lyon, war refugees were sent to live in the house with Roger. In addition to those sent from Lyon, many war victims found their way to Roger's front door. He never turned anyone away. Although he was very poor and food was sparse, Roger made do with whatever he could find, feeding his guests from the vegetables he grew in a small plot of farmed land on his property and from the milk of a cow he owned. Despite the fact that there were times when it seemed they would not survive, God always provided some form of nourishment for them.

From the very beginning, Roger prayed three times a day—sometimes in a chapel he made in a small room in the house, other times in a wooded area adjacent to the village. As many of the guests were Jewish, Roger never asked those who found refuge in Taizé to join him in prayer. During this time, though, Roger wrote a pamphlet that outlined his understanding of the monastic communal life. He wrote, "Every day let your work and rest be quickened by the Word of God; keep inner silence in all things and you will dwell in Christ; be filled with the spirit of the Beatitudes: joy, simplicity, and mercy."[9]

THE FIRST BROTHERS: 1942-1949

For a little over two years, Roger offered a safe haven for war refugees, even though the house was occasionally searched and he was warned that the Gestapo was suspicious of his activities. In November of 1942, Roger helped a refugee escape to Switzerland while on a trip to collect funds for his ministry. While he was gone, the Nazis raided the house in Taizé in search of refugees. A friend notified him of the activity in Taizé and strongly encouraged Roger to remain in Switzerland, because the Gestapo was waiting for him to return. He had no choice but to remain in Geneva in a small apartment that was owned by his parents.

During the following months, Roger finished his uncompleted thesis and published his small pamphlet outlining his understanding of Christian communal living. On April 30, 1943, Roger successfully defended his thesis, "The Ideal of the Monastic Life Before Saint Benedict and Its Conformity to the Gospels," and completed his degree. Although his academic work formally summarized most of his thoughts on the monastic life, it was his small pamphlet that gave birth to the first fraternity of brothers that would eventually become the Taizé community.

First, an agriculture student named Pierre Souvairan, who had read the pamphlet, knocked on Roger's door in Geneva and inquired about Roger's monastic ideals. Subsequently, a young theologian named Max Thurian also inquired about the pamphlet. The three of them formed a small brotherhood in the apartment in which Roger was living. Soon thereafter Daniel de Montmollin, another theology student, joined the three men, and they lived in Christian community together in Geneva for almost two years, dedicating themselves to a common life that included communally shared property, daily work and prayer, a common purse, and a life of celibacy. These provisional vows, however, were to be considered and renewed annually, as Brother Roger didn't want to risk entrapment in the possible minutia of static monasticism.

Early in the autumn of 1944, France was finally liberated from Nazi control, so Roger, Max, Pierre and Daniel were finally able to move to the house in Taizé. Life in the village was not easy, though, as the area was torn apart by the war. Towns and villages in the region were in shambles and many people were without homes. Anti-German sentiments grew in the area to the extent that some of the local women killed a young German Catholic priest in one of the prisoner-of-war camps located near Taizé. Although the war was over, the effects of the conflict remained for some time.

During the war, Brother Roger had ministered to Jewish refugees; after the war, in the midst of the tension, the four men began visiting the German prisoners-of-war and even gained permission from the authorities to invite them as guests to the house for dinner, though food was sparse. These actions eventually brought about intense criticism toward the brothers, but they remained faithful to their understanding of the gospel: to love their neighbor and to bring reconciliation—especially reconciliation between native inhabitants of the Burgundy region and the German war prisoners—in an area in desperate need of restoration.

Even in these earliest stages of formation with only four men, the fraternity of brothers at Taizé clearly affected the community through the simplicity of the gospel message they practiced. In addition to visiting prisoners, during this time the brothers cared for a group of boys orphaned by the war. Eventually, Genevieve, Brother Roger's youngest sister, moved to the area and cared for the boys in one of the neighboring villages. Since September 1940, the downtrodden, the poor and the marginalized have found peace and sanctuary in Taizé.

During this time, the brothers also undertook another venture: agricultural self-sustainability. Brother Pierre, the agriculturist, sought to rejuvenate the barren farmland that surrounded their property. By 1947 their little farm was not only providing nutritional sustenance for the brothers and their frequent guests but also producing enough food to offer financial stability to their community as well. This relative prosperity allowed them to welcome more guests as the years progressed.

These visitors, many of whom were Roman Catholic priests, took part in the devotional life of the brothers by praying with them three times a day. As the number of visitors grew, the room in which they prayed became overcrowded. All the while the old Romanesque church in the village remained vacant. It had not been used for regular worship in years. Brother Roger requested permission from the local ecclesial authority to use the church for daily prayers. Although permission was granted at first, after a few weeks the permission was retracted, and the brothers found themselves back in their upper-room chapel. After some time, Brother Roger again requested permission, but this time from the bishop of Autun, who turned the issue over to a higher authority in Paris. It eventually reached the desk of the future Pope John XXIII, Angelo Giuseppe Roncalli, who was the papal nuncio (the permanent diplomatic representative) in Paris at the time, and it was through his authority that the brothers were allowed to worship in the church. At last, on Pentecost 1948, the little village church was restored to a daily place of prayer.

In the same year, three Frenchmen decided to join the four Swiss brothers in their commitment to a Christ-centered communal life. Provisional vows, it was decided, were no longer sufficient for their community. Consequently, on Easter 1949 in the village church the seven men took the three traditional monastic vows: a life of celibacy, a life of common goods and a life under the authority of a prior, who was, not surprisingly, Brother Roger. At the time, this commitment was only significant for those seven men, despite the fact that "it marked the *first* time that the centuries-old monastic ideal had become a reality in the Churches of the Reformation."[10]

STRUGGLE FOR RECONCILIATION: 1949-1962

The Easter ceremony in 1949 brought about a key change in the communal life of those seven men that would prove to be of far greater significance in the years to come. In addition to establishing themselves as one of the first Protestant monastic orders in the history of the Judeo-Christian church, they also opened a pivotal door to a new type of monasticism, one which would eventually be characterized by ecumenism. For Brother Roger, ecumenism was less about tolerance and more about reconciliation. As a group of Protestant brothers, their small order did not attempt to return to Catholicism, nor did it expect the Catholic Church to fully acknowledge the legitimacy of their stake in the monastic tradition. Although they had been granted full use of the village church for daily prayers, Catholic worshipers were unable to join them. Permitting the brothers to use the old church for Protestant services was one thing, but deeming it acceptable for ecumenical worship was another. The brothers, nevertheless, were determined to seek reconciliation in the estranged relationship between Roman Catholics and Protestants. Now that their order was firmly established, Brother Roger began taking steps toward a more visible form of reconciliation.

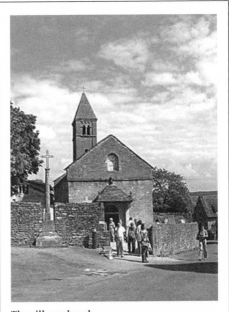

The village church

Thus, in 1949, through the encouragement of Cardinal Gerlier, the archbishop of Lyon who was adamantly supportive of the community's ecumeni-

cal efforts, Brother Roger and Brother Max traveled to Rome to seek an audience with Pope Pius XII. With only a short opportunity to share, Brother
Roger humbly made his request before the pope: "Leave a little way open,
even a very narrow one and define what you consider to be the essential
barriers—but leave a way forward. Do not close it altogether."[11] Although
the attempt initially seemed unsuccessful, years later Brother Roger's en-
treaty came to fruition, when the Holy Office bestowed each bishop with the
authority to grant Catholic participation in ecumenical gatherings. It was a
small step in the budding relationship that was developing between the Taizé
community and the papal authority in Rome.

By 1951, the community had increased to twelve brothers, and Brother
Roger felt they ought to be "signs of Christ's presence" outside their local
area. Consequently, two brothers moved to Montceau-les-Mines to work in
the mines. Although they were only twenty-five miles north of Taizé, the
two brothers lived in their new community and continued praying together
three times a day. They helped the local mining union struggle for their
rights, and before long, testimony of their efforts spread through the countryside. Montceau-les-Mines was only the first of many "fraternities" that
stemmed from the Taizé community.[12] Over the years, the brothers have
situated themselves amongst the poor of the world. From Calcutta, Bangla-
desh and the Philippines to Algeria, Brazil and even Hell's Kitchen in New
York City, the Brothers of Taizé have been an example of reconciliation and
peace to countless people.

Having established themselves in the monastic tradition in 1949, Brother
Roger felt it was time they adhered to a common rule. Thus, in the winter
of 1952-1953 Brother Roger withdrew from the community for a short period with the aim of writing a rule that incorporated only the most essential characteristics of their communal life. The Rule of Taizé that emerged,
then, unlike the rules it succeeded, focuses more on the general ethos of
how the brothers are to live together, rather than setting forth the exact
manner in which they're to conduct themselves in daily life. While the Rule
does offer simple guidelines for their communal life together, it allows for

considerable freedom and leaves ample room for personal discernment. Within the pages of the Rule are also various spiritual disciplines drawn from Scripture in which each brother endeavors to mature. Furthermore, Brother Roger included a description of the vows that each man takes in becoming a brother, the exhortation that's read at a new brother's profession and the actual commitments each brother professes. Although the original Rule that Brother Roger wrote is long out of print, an updated form exists today in the book *The Sources of Taizé*.[13]

In the years that followed the emergence of the Rule of Taizé, ecumenism weighed heavily on the hearts of the brothers. Each year the brothers saw an increase in the numbers of people visiting the community, and these visitors were no longer primarily from Protestant backgrounds—Taizé had caught the attention of many young Catholics as well.

Meanwhile, in Rome, progress toward reconciliation seemed almost unchanged. But 1958 marked a new era in Taizé's struggle for reconciliation. Pope Pius XII died, and his successor was none other than Angelo Giuseppe Roncalli, the papal nuncio who had given final permission for the brothers to pray in the village church. Before his inauguration, the archbishop of Lyon, Cardinal Gerlier, appealed to the new pope, John XXIII, to grant an audience to Brother Roger to discuss the role of ecumenism in the Catholic Church. Cardinal Gerlier was so successful in persuading the future pope to meet with Brother Roger that he and Brother Max departed for Rome soon thereafter. Only three days after John XXIII's inauguration, they were given a private audience with him, and to Brother Roger's delight their exchange was received much better than they had imagined it would be. "He was so interested," Brother Roger recalled, "and when we spoke of reconciliation he clapped his hands and exclaimed 'Bravo.'"[14] The meeting was just the beginning of a new relationship between the brothers and the many popes that followed. In fact, every year since that meeting, the brothers have had an audience with the pope. In the years that immediately followed, Pope John XXIII grew to cherish the Taizé community, and it was he who, upon seeing Brother Roger approaching him, declared, "Ah,

Taizé, that little springtime!"—a statement that has come to characterize the community even today.

In 1962, the Second Vatican Council began its first sessions, and to the credit of Pope John XXIII, Brother Roger and Brother Max were invited as observers. The blossoming relationship that had started only a few years previous, however, abruptly and sadly halted when the pope unexpectedly died on June 3, 1963, after almost a year of fighting stomach cancer. Although originally looked at as a stopgap pope, Angelo Giuseppe Roncalli will forever be remembered by the Brothers of Taizé for his benevolence and kindred spirit.

In addition to the advancements in ecumenism in the Roman Catholic Church, the early sixties brought significant changes for the Taizé community as well. The number of young people making pilgrimages to Taizé had reached a tipping point. No longer could they hold prayers in the little village church and accommodate their visitors. Although Brother Roger originally imagined their community to be a fellowship of twelve men living faithfully to the heart of the gospel, he realized that God had other plans in store. They faced the decision of whether or not they should build another church on a piece of land adjacent to the village. Brother Roger lamented the thought of moving out of the Romanesque church, but in the end, the brothers decided that a larger church had to be built.

It perhaps wasn't by coincidence that a young brother by the name of Denis was an architectural student before joining the community. In his last year of study, he designed the Church of Reconciliation with the community in mind, although without any anticipation that it would ever become a reality. The time was right to build, however, as the need was clearly present, a design was available, and the labor and funds to build the edifice appeared surprisingly through a German organization called Aktion Sühnezeichen. *Sühnezeichen,* which literally means "sign of atonement/reconciliation," was established in 1958 by Lothar Kreyssig to help rebuild areas that were destroyed during the war. This Christian-based effort enabled young Germans to offer signs of hope and reconciliation to those who suffered at the hands of their parents. They selected Taizé as one of their locations in France, perhaps in part because of the kindness the brothers showed to the German prisoners-of-war after the liberation of France. The connection went deeper than mere collaboration on a building project,

The Church of Reconciliation

though. Each day after the construction, these young Germans would join the brothers for evening prayers. Today, many of the brothers believe that German youth feel particularly drawn to Taizé because of this historical connection.

On August 6, 1962—the Feast of the Transfiguration—with many ecclesial dignitaries present, the new church was dedicated as a place of reconciliation and peace on earth. Newspaper journalists and film crews captured the event, wanting to know why so many young people were traveling to this little village to pray with a group of "Protestant monks." That's a question people continue to ask today.

5

A New Era of Reconciliation

Wait for the Lord, whose day is near.
Wait for the Lord: keep watch, take heart!

The church was complete, and it seemed that a new era had fallen upon their growing community. Brother Roger, however, actually lamented the building of the new church. Although he knew that their decision to build wasn't a rash one, to him the church seemed too big to pray in for most of the year. There were proportionately more people in Taizé around the holy days, like Easter and Pentecost, and during the warmer summer months, but he felt as though he was betraying his original vision for the community. Brother Roger wasn't trying to build something that would draw young people out of the proverbial woodwork. Rather, he was trying to live out the gospel in a small community of committed brothers. Thus, for a while, he felt disconcerted about what was happening to the community.

One day, however, while still feeling unsettled, he exited the new church and noticed a rainbow in the sky. In that instance, God transformed his perspective of the new church: "There is God's answer. This church will no immobilize us. It's an ark. It will be filled."[1] And less than a year later, the Church of Reconciliation was filled to capacity.

FOUNDATIONS FOR A PILGRIMAGE OF TRUST: 1962-1974

Young people continued to flock to Taizé, and the brothers tried desperately to accommodate them. It soon became clear to the brothers that building a church that could hold more young people meant adding other buildings to welcome visitors. Simple lodging and a dining area were constructed from 1962 to 1964, followed by the El Abiodh guesthouse in 1965. By this time, it was evident that the majority of visitors were young people, although the masses were interspersed with many adults. Brother Roger decided that an intentional effort to speak into the lives of these youth must become a priority. Consequently, in September of 1966, the Taizé community held their first intentional youth gathering. Although the original plan was to host only one meeting, the response to this gathering forced the brothers to consider how the young people fit into the future of the community. As a result, rather than organizing a single gathering during the summer of 1968, the brothers organized a series of summer meetings centered on the theme "believing."[2]

The following year was marked with world tragedies: shootings in Mexico City, demonstrations in Paris, and wars in Africa, the Middle East and Vietnam that surged on. In the midst of this chaos, Taizé stood as a beacon of hope and peace for young people. For the first time in the history of the community, a young Catholic doctor from Belgium took his vows as a brother; for many it was a welcome sign of reconciliation and a testimony to the growing ecumenism at Taizé. Soon after, more Roman Catholic brothers joined the community.

In February of 1970, the brothers found themselves surrounded by an unusually large number of people for that time of the year. Youth from forty-two different nations were present, and these young visitors began asking the brothers the question, "How can we take home what we have experienced here?" Although the brothers had no concrete answer to give, they heard the earnest pleas of the youth, and the seeds for the Council of Youth were planted.

In the months that followed, dialogue centered on reconciliation, unity and hope filled the air in Taizé. Then on Easter, before an audience of over twenty-five hundred young people from thirty different nations, a young man who presumably was in conversation with the brothers was given the microphone and said to the crowd: "The Risen Christ comes to quicken a festival in the innermost heart of man. He is preparing for us a springtime of the Church: a Church devoid of means of power, ready to share with all, a place of visible communion for all humanity. He is going to give us enough imagination and courage to open up a way of reconciliation. He is going to prepare us to give our lives so that man be no longer victim of man."[3] Then Brother Roger took the microphone and made the announcement, "We are going to hold a council of youth."[4] The silence after he spoke was deafening until the sound of a few clapping hands grew to a thunderous, almost earth-shattering roar. The zealous applause carried on longer than anyone could have imagined. That day marked the start of preparations for the Council of Youth, and for the next four years, young people met to discuss and pray about how to usher reconciliation into the world.

In 1971, almost a year after Brother Roger announced the idea for the Council of Youth, the brothers faced yet another difficult decision. Easter was quickly approaching, and they had received more requests to join them for the holy day than the Church of Reconciliation could accommodate. They could either write these young people to let them know that they couldn't welcome them to the community for Easter, or they could tear down the back of the church and erect a temporary circus tent to hold everyone. Although there was some reservation by a few brothers, the decision was made: the west wall must be torn down, despite the fact that a majestic stained-glass window was embedded in its concrete walls. With sledgehammers in hand, the brothers tore down the wall and in its stead erected an old red-and-white-striped circus tent.

For the remainder of the decade, they used the tent to welcome young people from all over the world, bringing it in whenever the need arose. Eventually, huge doors that could be raised replaced the gaping hole that the brothers created that year. Once again, the brothers saw the need to live with a malleable understanding of their life in Taizé. This mindset is what Brother Roger often referred to as living in the "dynamic of the provisional." Their overwhelming desire to welcome young people is clearly seen in their tireless efforts to adapt their plans and their calling to God's will.

The years leading up to the official opening of the Council of Youth on August 30, 1974, were rather indicative of Taizé's growing influence. In 1970, over twenty thousand young people ascended the hill throughout the year; by 1974 the numbers exploded to over sixty thousand pilgrims. The brothers were in utter disbelief. Over sixty thousand young people were traveling from across the globe to work and pray in their little village—a reality very different from Brother Roger's original vision for the community. August 30, 1974, marked the beginning of a new movement among the young pilgrims of Taizé, as Brother Roger invited the young people to begin to bring reconciliation across the globe. Every year since, young people have faithfully attempted to bring the peace and reconciliation they experience in Taizé to their nations, cities and neighborhoods. It would be impossible to measure the influence the Council of Youth has had on the world, but one thing is sure: because of it, young people around the globe are living their lives as bearers of hope, offering the reconciliation we find in Christ to those around them.

The year the Council of Youth officially began also brought an outpouring of public recognition for the Taizé community. On April 10, 1974, Brother Roger received the Templeton Prize, an award similar to the Nobel Peace Prize but given for spiritual contributions (the prize was awarded to Mother Teresa in 1973). The Templeton Prize carries with it the largest monetary award for this kind of merit. Brother Roger received thirty-four thousand pounds, which he promptly gave away to organizations working with immigrants in the United Kingdom, to people helping bring about religious reconciliation in Northern Ireland and to those helping the poor in South America. In addition to this prestigious prize, Brother Roger also received the German Peace Prize in the same year (other recipients include Albert Schweitzer [1951], Martin Buber [1953] and Paul Tillich [1962]). Although Brother Roger never wanted notoriety, the world had finally taken notice of their community.

Since it was clear they had a captive audience, Brother Roger began writing a letter to young people around the world in an effort to bring a message of hope to help sustain them on their pilgrimage of trust on the earth. He continued to write these letters each year until his unexpected death in 2005. Since that time, the new prior of Taizé, Brother Alois, has continued in this tradition.

SETTLING DOWN: 1975-2005

In the years that followed the opening of the Council of Youth, the brothers developed the notion of a "Pilgrimage of Trust" which literally took the brothers and many young people across the globe. From Europe and Asia to Africa and the Americas, the brothers sought to bring a message of hope to the poor. Additionally, during that time many church dignitaries visited the community in hopes of understanding why young people were so attracted to Taizé.

Even Mother Teresa visited Taizé during the month of August in 1976. In turn, Brother Roger took a group of young people to Calcutta to minister to those under Mother Teresa's care. While in Calcutta, five brothers and ten young people lived among the poor. For five weeks they worked, prayed and slept in poverty, helping Mother Teresa in any way she saw fit. It was here, in the midst of the poverty, disease and utter despondency, that Brother Roger and Mother Teresa composed a prayer together:

Oh God, the father of all,
You ask every one of us to spread
Love where the poor are humiliated,

Joy where the Church is brought low,

And reconciliation where people are divided . . . ,

Father against son, mother against daughter,

Husband against wife,

Believers against those who cannot believe,

Christians against their unloved fellow Christians.

You open this way for us, so that the wounded body of Jesus Christ,
your Church, may be leaven of Communion for the poor of the earth
and in the whole human family.[5]

While in one of Mother Teresa's hospitals, Brother Roger was drawn to
an eight-week-old Indian baby. One of the sisters informed him that without
help the baby would die very soon. He knew he had to help, so he adopted
her and brought her back to France to receive proper medical treatment. She
was named Marie Louise Sonaly—after Brother Roger's grandmother—
and lived with his sister, Genevieve, in the village. In the years that followed
she often accompanied Brother Roger in his travels.

Taizé was at the height of its unexpected growth, and despite the success
in the brothers' quest to plant seeds of reconciliation abroad, they faced
the continued challenge of how to welcome these transient young people
through the revolving door of their community. For example, every part of
the liturgy was sung or read in French, which immensely troubled Brother
Roger. How could they truly invite these young people to join them in
prayer when the pilgrims were from so many countries with so many different languages? The mid to late 1970s therefore mark an essential shift in the
Taizé prayers, one that I will explore in more depth in chapter eight. Before
this period of growth, the prayers of the Taizé community looked strikingly
different than they do today.

Throughout the 1980s, the brothers continued to live among the poor in
other nations. They held European meetings every year in a different city.
Pope John Paul II even made a visit to Taizé in 1986. Numbers continued to
increase, climbing to over two thousand people during some of the summer

weeks. Numbers were never important to the brothers; they only desired to welcome those pilgrims who joined them for a week of prayer. Up to that time, most of young people who visited them were from Catholic or Protestant traditions. Although there were a small number of Orthodox Christians represented, Eastern Europeans and Russians had very little access or opportunity to travel to Taizé. That dynamic changed in 1989, however.

On November 9, 1989, the East German government announced that East Germans were permitted to enter West Berlin. Almost overnight Taizé felt the impact of that historic announcement. The number of young people swelled, eventually reaching over 6,000 during the summer weeks and up to 100,000 over the year. Finally, the three traditions of Christianity could freely pray together in one location. To welcome the first-time Eastern Europeans to their community, the brothers expanded the Church of Reconciliation and erected several onion-shaped domes on the roof. They hoped that Eastern Orthodox pilgrims would exit the buses and feel as though they were home.

Before the end of the year, the brothers organized a European meeting in Poland—the first of its kind in Eastern Europe. In the years that followed, ecumenism flourished in Taizé, and while they continued to evaluate the functioning of their community, their daily activities became more established. They continued to welcome young people, produce pottery and pray three times a day. More brothers moved to poor areas in cities around the world, and they continued to hold large Taizé gatherings worldwide. In other words, life carried on.

In fact, during the last decade of Brother Roger's life, the provisional nature of their communal life, which had once so readily characterized Taizé, became more settled—not because the brothers desired permanency but rather because this community of brothers continued faithfully living out their calling among the poor and with the thousands of young pilgrims who traversed to their village each year. Over the following years, many trips were taken—too many to highlight—and more awards were bestowed. It seemed that Brother Roger and his community had found their place in the ever-expanding ecumenical world. In short, life was good for the Taizé community.

UNEXPECTED TRAGEDY: 2005

Then without warning, Brother Roger's life was taken. No one could have predicted that he would pass on to the next life in the manner in which he did. Although he was ninety years old and had a difficult time seeing and walking, Brother Roger continued to touch the lives of pilgrims that made their way to Taizé. At the time of his death, the Catholic Church was holding its 2005 World Youth Day in Cologne, Germany. About four hundred thousand young people from two hundred countries gathered in various locations around Cologne during the week, and more than one million came for the weekend celebration. Many of the Taizé brothers were near Cologne at the time holding prayer services in Bonn.

Due to the fact that World Youth Day occurred in mid August, only twenty-five hundred young people were present in the Taizé community when the attack took place. When news of Brother Roger's death reached Cologne, however, close to fifteen thousand young people and friends of the community made their way to the little village by the end of the week. Countless church dignitaries joined the masses for his funeral a week after his death. With newspapers, video crews and reporters scattered throughout the crowd, the world witnessed the impact of Brother Roger's life.

His message of reconciliation was heard that day as Brother Alois, the new prior of the community, read a prayer of forgiveness: "God of goodness, we entrust to your forgiveness Luminiţa Solcan who, in an act of sickness, put an end to the life of Brother Roger. With Christ on the cross we say to you: Father, forgive her, she does not know what she did." The Church of Reconciliation was packed full of young people; the overflow had to stand in one of the fields and watch the funeral on a Jumbotron. It rained that day—or, more accurately, it poured; it was if the heavens wept for the loss of Brother Roger's life. Then, just as the funeral was ending, the clouds broke open and intense beams of light filled the sky. Brother Roger was with his Creator.

The week that followed the funeral was surprisingly normal. The prayers continued on their regular schedule, as did the communal work. The Bible Introductions and sharing groups met the very next day. The only real difference was that there was an aura of peace that transcended human understanding—or perhaps it only felt that way, because we assume that tragedy breeds calamity. It was quite common to hear other pilgrims ask, "Have you seen the brothers cry?" "Are the brothers mourning Brother Roger's death?" While I'm sure they mourned his death, each in his own way, their reaction made it clear that Taizé is an entirely different type of community. In other words, when the ethos of a community is so imbued with the longing for reconciliation, even in the face of senseless evil, forgiveness and consequently peace can reside.

TAIZÉ TODAY

Since the time of Brother Roger's death, not much has changed in the community. At least, nothing significant has changed. As I mentioned earlier, subtle adaptations will always take place at Taizé; it's part of the provisional nature that personifies the community. Several brothers have commented that the pace of the community has increased since that night in August

Brother Roger's funeral

2005. For the last decade of his life, Brother Roger wasn't as quick or nimble as he was in his youth. Projects, trips to other countries and planning for the future therefore all took a bit longer. Everything simply slowed down. In fact, one brother said that in the fifteen years before

Brother Roger's death, the church choir area retained its appearance longer than any other arrangement in the history of the community.

This deceleration of community life during Brother Roger's last ten years was more difficult for some brothers than others. Even in his seventies, Brother Roger was full of life, and everything and everybody "went at a cracking pace." As with all things in life, however, there are different seasons. Many of the brothers reflect upon the last decade as a time of preparation. The projects that were on hold for the future are now being implemented. It is springtime in the community again, and its energy is refreshing for all.

The most significant change for many is the face of a new prior. Brother Alois succeeded Brother Roger as the new prior immediately upon his death. Born on June 11, 1954, in Nördlingen, Germany, Alois Löser grew up in Stuttgart. Raised in the Roman Catholic tradition, Alois was an altar boy and a youth leader in his local parish in Stuttgart. He found his way to Taizé during his late teenage years. After spending some time as a permanent, he decided to explore the possibility of a lifelong commitment as a brother.

Thus, in 1974, the same year the Council of Youth officially began, the twenty-year-old Alois entered the community as a brother of Taizé. Four years later, he made his life commitment. In 1998, Brother Roger officially appointed Alois to be his successor (he had already discreetly selected him twenty years before) and, in January 2005, announced to the community that Brother Alois would begin his post before the end of the year. In many ways, Brother Alois simply picked up where Brother Roger left off, which I'm sure would have been the way Brother Roger would have wanted it.

From its humble beginnings when young Roger welcomed his first refugee into his new home during the war to the height of its growth in the early 1990s when over 100,000 young people ascended the hill, Brother Roger's earnest longing for reconciliation could be seen. Without a doubt, the history of the community is a testimony to both God's divine guidance and the humility of the human spirit to seek after God's will. Although Taizé has, in its own right, come of age in a postmodern world, only time will tell whether or not its passion for hope and peace will sustain its appeal for young people in the decades to come. There is, however, one thing that's certain: no matter how many young people continue to make Taizé their spiritual home or the starting point of their spiritual pilgrimage, the Brothers of Taizé will continue living faithfully to the heart of the gospel found in the words of Jesus Christ. They have never judged their own faithfulness by the world's perception of their community's success. Perhaps that's because the brothers understand that God calls all of us to be faithful, not successful.

6

The Brothers of Taizé

The kingdom of God is justice and peace and joy in the Holy Spirit.
Come, Lord, and open in us the gates of your kingdom.

On my last research trip to Taizé, I had the opportunity to take my wife, Shannon, and my six-year-old son, Judah. Although they were both excited to finally experience for themselves what I had been researching for the better part of two years, Judah couldn't wait to actually see the brothers. Despite falling asleep the first night in the evening prayers (in all fairness, we had just arrived and he had been up for over twenty-four hours with nothing more than two little catnaps), he was enthralled by the prayer times and, in particular, the brothers.

Judah always wanted to get "good seats" (like father, like son). For Judah, however, this translated into "somewhere where he can see the brothers." He enjoyed watching them walk into the church from behind the little wall and take their seats, and he was quick to point out when they were standing up to leave. The second day we were there, during one of the chants, he leaned over to me and said, "Daddy, are they monks or are they brothers?"

Failing miserably to contain my smile, I quietly whispered back to him, "I think they prefer to be called 'brothers.'"

Despite the innocence of his question, Judah's interest and fascination with the brothers is actually quite normal. During most visitors' first few times in the prayers, they can't help but stare in awe of the beauty of what this community has come to represent: an unwavering commitment to live out the gospel through a communal existence. This type of commitment is so rare in our culture that when we encounter it, we find ourselves dumbfounded. Even more so, the sheer simplicity and beauty of the church, in conjunction with the brothers' white habits, conjure up our hidden curiosity with the monastic tradition.

Interestingly enough, the brothers don't see themselves as extraordinary men with a heightened proclivity for theology or spirituality but rather as simple men who are merely seeking to live their lives faithfully in Christ. In many ways, they are quite normal. They laugh and joke, they're up to date on world events, and some even read popular literature. I was surprised to find out that two of the brothers are fans of Anne Lamott, an esteemed author around my home. In essence, the Brothers of Taizé are ordinary people who have simply made an extraordinary commitment—and through that commitment, young people around our world are experiencing Christ. With that said, let's take a look at what makes this community of brothers tick and, in doing so, hopefully answer some of those dubious inquiries concerning their public and private lives.

For the record, I confirmed my answer to Judah's question (concerning what the brothers prefer to be called) in an interview later that week. It's true; they prefer to be called "brothers," as this label both clarifies their monastic vocation for the world and also links them more closely to the language used in Scripture. Within a Judeo-Christian context, monks are more closely associated with Catholic monastic orders, an association that could prove confusing for those who understand them as an ecumenical monastery. The brothers do, however, consider themselves *in* the monastic tradition, even though Brother Roger was wary of calling Taizé a monastic community. They are not seeking distinction for the mere sake of distinction but instead desire to be associated with the great history of Christian monasticism. As those traditions did before them, they take vows and live under a common rule. Unlike traditional monasteries, however, they welcome, lodge and often feed up to six thousand young pilgrims a week. In short, they are brothers, in the monastic tradition, living in a communal and ecumenical fellowship, who happen to minister to a lot of young people.

It's worth noting that when someone becomes a brother, he retains his specific denomination, tradition and ordination status. While a few Catholic priests and Protestant pastors are sprinkled throughout the membership, most of the brothers come from the laity of both traditions. What does change, however, is their vocation. The brothers come from all sorts of professions: some were doctors, musicians and teachers, while others were architects, theologians and engineers. Regardless of experience, though, when new brothers come into the community they are given the opportunity to try many different jobs. Brother Roger was insistent that no brother get pinned down into doing one task just because his training or education was in a particular field. This means that a former teacher could find himself painting pottery or an engineer helping arrange housing for the pilgrims. There is no job too big or small, or of more or less value in Taizé. Each job is a function of the whole, and each brother has a part.

One of the most common questions I've been asked is, "How many brothers are there?" I can only answer with the same vagueness in which I was answered when I asked several brothers the same question: around one hundred, or maybe even closer to one hundred and ten. I was rather amused that the multiple answers to this question came with a settled ambiguity. While I'm positive there's a definite number within a book of records somewhere in the little village, I found it rather refreshing that it wasn't a point of boasting. It's simply not an important figure for the brothers. What's more important and a little less ambiguous is that there are over twenty-five nations represented in their fellowship, making the Brothers of Taizé not only one of the largest ecumenical orders in the monastic tradition but also the most diverse.

In truth, part of why it's difficult to calculate the number of brothers is because many of them are living among the poor in other countries. One brother estimated that sixty to seventy brothers live in residence at any given point, with that number climbing up to eighty during the busiest periods of the summer. The influx throughout the year is not only due to various brothers living overseas, but also because many brothers are away preparing for future meetings, visiting families or meeting with other contacts. While there are some brothers who have remained outside the walls of Taizé for the majority of their monastic life, others hardly leave. There is no rotational system that mandates who goes here or there, and there are no precedents that dictate what ought to happen; rather, each year situations are dealt with on a case-by-case basis.

This manner of organization means that each brother might not always return to the same room after a long absence. While in Taizé, however, each brother always has his own room. This provides them each with a little space where they can retreat to pray in private. Many of the brothers live in the original house that Brother Roger purchased in 1940, although they have divided many of the rooms into smaller rooms as numbers grew. Furthermore, they converted many of the buildings directly adjacent to the house (the wine press, the barn, etc.) into housing to accommodate the growing number of brothers.

Interestingly enough, the brothers' house and rooms are filled with secondhand, picked-up-by-the-side-of-the-road furniture. Apparently, in the 1950s and 1960s local farmers and homeowners throughout the Burgundy countryside were modernizing their houses. Many threw out their old kitchen hutches, chests of drawers and armoires. Brother Roger went around and offered to buy them. Many of the pieces he purchased for next to nothing or got for free. He thought it a shame that these majestic wardrobes, which were used for decades (some for over a hundred years), were devalued as nothing more than firewood. Because of these recovered pieces the brothers haven't had to purchase much furniture. As one of the brothers shared this story with me, I looked around the room we were in at the various trunks and cabinets. Many pieces were simple, but others were adorned with hand-carved trim and decorative paneling. Ironically, most of these pieces would now be considered quite valuable antiques.

BECOMING A BROTHER

Every year several young men consider what it would be like to be a brother, although some pursue it with more determination than others. The process of becoming a brother is not easy, and it involves careful discernment for both the individual and the community of brothers as a whole. Many people want to know what it takes to become a brother of Taizé. Although the specifics of the journey are unique to each person, there are general phases through which each brother travels.

It's safe to say that for most of the brothers the process began with a personal pilgrimage to Taizé. Among the 100,000 pilgrims that visit the community each year, there are always young men who feel drawn to remain in Taizé for a longer period. If a young man experiences this desire, he must first approach one of the brothers about staying in Taizé as a volunteer, or what has come to be known as a "permanent." The brother will ask the young man why he wants to stay and for how long he's hoping to extend his time. Some young men only want to stay for a month to spend more time praying about life decisions, while others may request to stay for a year. In many cases, the young men who are seriously considering a life in the brotherhood end up staying in Taizé for one or two years.

During this time in Taizé, the male permanents live in a building behind La Morada, the meetinghouse adjacent to the brothers' home. Many of them also work in La Morada, assisting in the communication between visitors and the brothers. Occasionally, the male permanents are invited to the brothers' common midday meal. The young men are also able to join various brothers for dinner, which is not a communal meal. Although they don't actually live with the brothers, of all the various groups of people in Taizé, the young men shadow the brothers the most closely. They're able to

observe both the blessings and challenges of living as a brother in an ecumenical monastic community.

While volunteering, each young permanent gets a "contact brother" with
whom he will meet on a regular basis for prayer and discussion. It is through
these meetings that the discernment process begins. The contact brother
helps the young man determine what he is searching for in life and understand why he is drawn to communal living. For some new brothers, this
discernment process is a clear one; for others it takes much longer. At some
point during this process, however, it becomes clear for all—both the young
man and the brothers—whether or not his future lies in the community. If
both sense it is right, the young man makes the decision to enter the brotherhood. Once the decision is made, the young man is given the white prayer
robe and a simple ceremony is held during the Saturday evening prayers,
after which the man is considered a brother of Taizé.

Although in appearance the new brothers look just like the other brothers, in reality they are considered "young brothers." This designation is not
meant to create classes of brothers, but rather to allow for a formational period, which can last anywhere between three to five years. During this time
the young brothers undergo training in biblical and theological studies, but
the majority of their formation comes through actually living in the community of brothers. The young brothers continue to meet with their original
contact brothers, who act as mentors. When the time is right, which is different for each brother, a life commitment is made by the young brother.

At this point, the brother takes the three traditional monastic vows and
receives the life commitment ring. The brothers wear these rings, which
are similar to traditional wedding rings, on the ring finger of their left
hand as a reminder of their solemn commitment to Christ and to the community of brothers in which they will remain for the rest of their lives. I
have included in appendix B the life commitment vows that every brother
who intends to remain in Taizé for the remainder of his life must make before the assembly. The commitments made during this ceremony are not
one-sided, however. Each brother who has taken these vows is reminded

of his own covenant in the community. In many ways, the process leading up to a life commitment by a young brother of Taizé is very similar to that of traditional marriage commitments.

Consider how we date in Western society. We meet someone we're drawn to, much like a young man might feel on his first pilgrimage to Taizé. Then, in the same way we decide we'd like to continue dating the person in order to get to know them better, a young man decides to volunteer for a longer period. If we, however, decide at this point that the relationship isn't going to work, we break up. Similarly, many of the young permanents decide to leave after spending a few months in the community. They determine, perhaps, that a long-term commitment isn't for them, or that it's simply time to move on. If both sides of a relationship feel positively about where the relationship is going, though, marriage is considered and an engagement ring acts as a symbol of that promised commitment.

In addition to the ring, the brothers' white prayer robes act as an engagement ring, as a visible symbol of their commitment to the community and to the monastic life. Just as the engagement ring serves as an outward sign of a couple's intention to marry, the white habit is an indication of the young brother's intention to take the life vows. Then, on a blessed day, just as the bride and groom exchange rings to symbolize their lifelong marriage commitments, the young brother takes his vows and receives a ring to signify his commitment to the monastic life in Taizé. Though it's not a perfect analogy, dating and marriage in the West offer a good comparison for the commitment the brothers take in their vows.

That's not to say that no brother has ever left the community. In fact, a small number of life-commitment brothers have left over the years. But more often it's the young brothers who decide to leave before taking their life commitments. It's difficult to pinpoint why a brother would leave after being in the community. Some realize that it isn't where they were supposed to be or that it was just a part of their larger journey. Others might have felt that God was moving them on.

The village of Taizé as you leave the community

In addition to brothers who've chosen to leave over the years, eleven brothers have died. While a few are buried in other parts of the world, most are buried next to the old village church. This is where Brother Roger is buried, and during the afternoons in Taizé, countless visitors wander down to the church to pay their respects at Brother Roger's grave. A simple wooden cross, engraved with "F. Roger," was erected at the head of the plot. It's a small reminder of the sacrificial commitment he made to bring about the reconciliation Christ procured on the cross—a commitment that he will be remembered for always.

THE MONASTIC LIFE

Without question, there's a natural flow of life present in Taizé. Many join. A few leave. Some die. In the midst of this normal life cycle, though, we find ordinary men who have an extraordinary determination to live faithfully, like their first prior did, as a sign of reconciliation. Within this normal life flow the brothers have their own daily rhythm of life that exemplifies several of the intentional characteristics of the community.

At the center of the brothers' common life is prayer. The community's existence is infused with this ancient church practice. Not only do the brothers formally gather for prayer three times a day, but, according to the Rule, they also seek time outside of common prayer for personal devotion. For some this prayer time is carved out of the early morning hours before anyone is up; for others it's late at night, after they retire to their personal quarters. Some brothers even find time during the day to step away from the masses and seek after God alone. Finding time during the day, however, is a challenge of its own for the brothers, as their days are consumed by at least one of three areas that keep the community functioning: household, work and welcome.

Even when the brothers are not dressed in their white prayer robes, you can usually spot them around the community. There's a joke among the visitors that all the brothers dress the same: socks and sandals, chinos, and a button-down oxford shirt. If the weather is colder, they'll wear a fitted sweater over the shirt. They dress simply, but in a classic European style.

Just like you and me, the brothers have daily household responsibilities. Clothing must still be washed, meals prepared and their houses cleaned. They also have two dogs that have to be fed, cleaned up after and groomed. Most of these tasks are completed by the brothers themselves, not visitors.

There are a few brothers who are responsible for cooking for the community of brothers—both for the common lunch and for dinner. After the midday prayers, the brothers congregate either in the large common dining room or, when the weather is warm, under a long white canopy situated at the back of their property. The canopy was erected in recent years, because the trees that once lined this dining area needed to be cut down. The picture created by the brothers sitting and eating at this long table on a cool, sunny autumn day is idyllic, to say the least. For dinner, the brothers can pick up a plate from the kitchen and eat their meal there or casually gather in the common dining room. Occasionally, the brothers will eat with the pilgrims and the permanents, or meet with visitors for dinner in El Abiodh. Although the brothers don't help cook the meal when they eat outside of their own home, they always help with the clean-up.

While my family and I were having dinner with two brothers one evening, I was amazed by one of their responses as the meal was ending. He said, "I'll wash the dishes, if you'd like to dry." Even after my appeal to him of "Let us do the dishes. That way, you can get ready for prayers," he responded, "If we all work together, it won't take long." The old proverb "Many hands make light work" rang true that evening, as it does every evening there. For the brothers, servanthood is a lifestyle. Whether in the larger community or in their home, they share the workload. They have no expectation that others will serve them. Brother Roger understood himself to be the first of many servants, and the brothers carry on this tradition. This is just one way they bear one another's burdens. The household duties, however, are only one of three areas in which the brothers work each day.

The second area of their daily life centers on their artisanship, or the way they make money. In the 1940s, Brother Roger decided that the community would not take donations for the livelihood of the brothers. Even if a brother receives an inheritance from a family member, the money is given to the poor. Every cent that is collected in Taizé either goes toward the room and board and welcome for the pilgrims, or to a charity called Operation Hope.[1] As mentioned earlier, the brothers live entirely from the sales of the Exposition. What originally began in the hands of Brother Daniel during the late 1940s (literally by his hands, as he was a potter) has turned into the single greatest source of income for the brothers. Behind La Morada sits a pottery shop where the brothers make both the pottery and the enamel pendants.

In order to make the pottery, they bring in local clay by the truckload. It's mixed and formed into smaller, workable units. Then they press each unit into a mold, harden it in the kiln, hand-paint it and fire it again. Although the machines press every piece, each step of the process is controlled by the work of a brother's hand. Despite the fact that the work is arduous, the cost of the pottery is really quite reasonable, unless you want a one-of-a-kind hand-sculpted piece. Brother Daniel can still be seen retiring to his old shop and sitting for hours at the potter's wheel perfecting a work of art. Visitors can purchase his original pottery in the Exposition, but the cost for these pieces is substantially higher.

Before 2007, they didn't allow anyone who wasn't a brother in the pottery shop. Even the young men who volunteered and lived next to the pottery workshop were unable to watch the brothers at work. Every few years in this region of France, however, several local potteries open their doors to the public for visitation, and although the brothers had never participated before, in the spring of 2007 they decided to take part. Thus, for the first time in the history of the community, nonbrothers were permitted to enter the shop. During my final research trip for this book, I was given the opportunity to tour their shop. It was an impressive operation, to say the least. During my short tour, I witnessed a dozen or so brothers assiduously creating various pieces, and painting each with care.

I was also privileged to see several brothers meticulously painting the enamel pendants, each of which is crafted by hand. Beyond the Taizé dove-cross pendants, the brothers started making doughnut- (only flat) and leaf-shaped pendants, each with different designs on them. Each design was inspired by a specific Scripture and comes with a card with the verse on it. These pendants are among the most-purchased items in the Exposition, as they are inexpensive and easy to take home without fear of breakage.

Although almost every brother has spent time in the pottery shop, there is much work to be done outside of it too, particularly in welcoming and preparing for up to six thousand young people a week. Coordinating the food and accommodations for the visitors is perhaps the most difficult work for the brothers. Since the early 1950s, they've faced the constantly growing challenge of how to care for the pilgrims who come to their community. With the massive surge in the early 1970s, they experimented with different formulas until they found an effective means of demonstrating hospitality to the young people. Today, many of the brothers spend the good part of their day serving in some capacity of welcoming pilgrims. Whether by answering emails, confirming reservations, or coordinating the room and board, the brothers are involved in each step of the process.

In addition to these duties, several brothers must plan the liturgy for each prayer time. Chants must be selected with careful consideration of the nations represented in Taizé each week. Music must be coordinated. Scripture readings must be chosen and placed by the doors of the church before each prayer time. Other brothers must prepare and lead the Bible Introductions, meet with visitors and offer guidance to the young men who volunteer. Even with all of these tasks considered, there are brothers who also plan for the European meetings and gatherings in other countries. With all of these responsibilities that need to be done, "free time" is a luxury the brothers do not generally afford themselves. In a day and age where such high value is placed on "personal space," "down time" and "leisure activities," it's overwhelming to think about living with such intentionality that free time is a rarity.

For better or for worse, this is the life of the brothers. None of them entered the community hastily or on a whim. It was clear from my conversations with the brothers that they love the communal life of Taizé, even with the occasional hardship that accompanies a life together. While most pilgrims don't really get to experience the daily challenges of living in Christian community, there are other groups of people in Taizé besides the brothers that do.

7

Permanents, Sisters and les Jeunes

Behüte mich, Gott, ich vertraue dir, (Keep me, O God, for I trust in you,)
du zeigst mir den Weg zum Leben. (You show me the path of life.)
Bei dir ist Freude, Freude in Fülle. (With you there is fullness of joy.)

If we could hover over the Taizé community and watch the various interactions that transpire, we might be persuaded to believe that the community is larger than the hundred or so brothers that make this little French village their permanent home. In some ways this is true. While the Brothers of Taizé are the only official members of the community, several other groups of people there help make Taizé what it is today. Although these other groups are transient in nature—sometimes only spending a week on the hill—during their time in Taizé, they quickly become part of a larger community.

The brothers themselves acknowledge the multifaceted nature of their community. One brother even asserted that Taizé was a little glimpse of the church-at-large: "It's like an onion, with its different layers, but all still a part of the whole." This analogy can especially be seen in the daily life of the community.

Though there are different groups, everyone exists together and collectively bears witness to the unity of the church. One brother commented, "The idea would be that we all live together in one week, as one community . . . that we are open to one another." This is the brothers' hope for the future.

The "Permanents"

If the brothers are the heart of the community, the diverse and ever-changing crowd of young people known by thousands as the "permanents" is definitely the muscle of Taizé. These young people are the reason the brothers can welcome over 100,000 pilgrims a year. While in English the term *permanent* means "lasting or unchanged," in French, *les permanent* literally means a union or party official or worker, conveying the notion of a paid administrative member of a staff. Ironically, neither definition really captures the essence of permanents at Taizé, as they are not long-term residents nor paid workers. They are, in a word, volunteers. They are young people who live for a determined period in the community to help organize the larger pilgrim population. The number of permanents depends highly on the time of the year, with more during the summer and sometimes only a few during the winter months. During the summer, the community can see up to fifty male permanents and up to seventy female permanents.

Without their help, the broader community of pilgrims could not function effectively. Although the brothers have designed and established an infrastructure for the pilgrims, the permanents keep the wheels moving. They confirm the online reservations that pilgrims receive before their journey. They coordinate the welcome procedures on a daily basis. They head up the work teams of pilgrims each week. Each meal is prepared, cooked, transported, distributed and cleaned up under the leadership of these hard-working young people, who often are younger than many of the pilgrims.

The permanents' jobs span the entire expanse of the communal life of Taizé. Unless there's a problem they would need to consult one of the brothers or sisters about, they do their jobs without supervision. This lack of oversight isn't due to the neglect of leadership on the brothers' part; on the contrary, it's due to the great level of trust the brothers extend to the permanents. They trust them to do their jobs with competence and diligence. For some of the young permanents, it's the first time they've ever really experienced what it's like to have someone trust them.

A young man from Poland named Michał recalled for me his first week as a Taizé permanent:

> I remember I was here as a permanent, for one month a few years ago. I was given a tractor. The brother wanted me to drive it and to take some things from the village and bring it to another location. That was for me a big sign of trust. I have never before driven a tractor and I was just given this chance, even before going around here to try it out. They confided in me and gave some tasks and that's how they trust. They trust young people and give them some responsibilities. They don't say, "Ahhh . . . you've never worked in press, you can't write an article or a text on something." They just give them the paper and tell them, "Maybe you can write about it."

For the brothers, trusting the permanents is crucial to the ethos in Taizé. The young permanents rise to the challenge of managing the community because they want to honor the trust that the brothers place in them.

The permanents receive no pay or compensation for their labor. The brothers provide food, lodging and spiritual guidance in exchange for their work. Moreover, the young people have very little free time. In fact, for many years the permanents had few afternoons or days off, but in recent years the brothers finally implemented a rotation system

Signpost to the community

to allow the permanents to take an afternoon off to go for a walk or ride a bike into Cluny. This opportunity gives them a chance to be alone and recharge and was definitely a welcomed and needed change for all of the permanents.

The communal life cycle of the permanents is quite different from that of the brothers, because most of them are not intending to remain in the community for the rest of their lives. Often young people decide they'd like to become a permanent after spending only one week in the community. If they feel this inclination, they must first meet with one of the brothers to explain why they'd like to volunteer and how long they intend on staying. They both agree on a starting date and the duration of their stay, and then the young person returns to the community at the agreed-upon day. Occasionally, if the young person is free and the community needs the help, the new permanent will start immediately.

As I've mentioned, the male permanents either sleep in a building behind La Morada or, if they're staying less than a month, in one of the houses in the village. The female permanents begin in a dormitory directly behind El Abiodh, but if they remain in Taizé and space opens up they might move to one of the rooms in El Abiodh. Outside of the work that they share, the male and female permanents have very little direct contact with one another. Each permanent does meet with either a brother or a sister (whom I will describe in more detail below) on a regular basis though.

Although permanents agree to stay in the community for a specific length of time, sometimes this changes. On occasion, a permanent feels that life in Taizé is not what they're looking for and leaves early. Others request to stay longer when their time ends. Depending on the situation, the brothers may or may not extend their stay, as they want what is best for each permanent. For various reasons, sometimes this means letting a permanent go.

The social dynamic that surrounds the permanents is an interesting one. Sometimes they're among the friendliest people in the community, other times some of them act as if your presence in the community bothers them. Having experienced both extremes each time I've been in Taizé, I decided to ask both the brothers and a group of the permanents why there was such a range in the disposition of these young people. The brothers, who have watched endless cycles of permanents over the past few decades, have noticed that the attitudes of the permanents change the longer they are in the community. In the first few weeks of a permanent's stay, they are often very friendly. For many of them, it feels like an extended week in Taizé. They're excited to meet new people and learn how the community functions, and their new role connects them to the community in a different way, which makes them feel special. It's almost a honeymoon stage for the permanents. Everything seems perfect. For the permanents who only stay for a month, the honeymoon phase never ends. By the time they settle into their new responsibilities, the prospect of their departure is upon them. The permanents who stay longer than a month, however, experience the end of this honeymoon phase. The work at Taizé is hard and demanding on the volunteers, and eventually it takes its toll.

During a permanent's second month, they realize that they can't continue emotionally investing themselves in every friend they meet, week after week, only to have them leave. They can only collect so many emails before their "Taizé friendship book" is so full they don't remember who's who. In other words, there is a calcification that occurs in permanents the longer they stay. They realize that people come and people go; meanwhile their work in the community remains the same. The excitement of the new experience wears off, and the realities of living in an imperfect community begin to set in.

When I spoke with the permanents, they confirmed this shift. Several of them commented, "We get tired of making new friends to only have them leave." They all expressed

One of the village houses

this sentiment with regret, albeit resolved regret. One added, "What else can we do, we are here for much longer. They [the pilgrims] come and go, but we remain." If I understood them correctly, they didn't want to appear standoffish, but they also really didn't know how to deal with this ever-changing social dynamic.

According to one brother, another aspect of this social dynamic that affects how permanents respond to others centers on the permanents' longing to feel special or unique in the community. Often when young people go from being visitors to permanents they begin to act differently toward the pilgrims. Part of this change is normal, because each new permanent experiences an identity shift in their relationship to the community. The brothers hope that a spirit of servanthood characterizes this new identity, but it doesn't always happen that way. One brother intimated, "Anything which is exclusive—that we are special—is contrary to the spirit of Taizé. Even though people want to feel a bit more like 'I belong more than the people who are here for a week,' we don't want that really." It's not that the brothers don't want the permanents to feel special, because it's very clear that they are a unique part of the community. Nonetheless, they don't want them to carry themselves as if they're above the pilgrims who are only there for a week. After all, both the visitors and the permanents are on this lifelong spiritual pilgrimage together. Another brother reaffirmed this, saying, "They are special and it's important that we affirm that, but at the end of the day, there is no difference between someone who is here as a permanent and someone who is here for a week."

Thus, even in Taizé, young people struggle to find their place in the world. Part of the process of helping these young permanents "find themselves" is the guidance given by the brothers and sisters. Just as the brothers guide the male permanents, the sisters help oversee the female permanents, which creates a unique opportunity for the sisters who have made Taizé their home.

THE SISTERS

During a pilgrim's daily routine in Taizé, it would be impossible not to notice the handful of sisters serving in the community. It should be noted from the start, however, that while there are many women around the Taizé community who have taken monastic vows of their own, none of them are "Taizé Sisters." People often incorrectly refer to them as "The Sisters of Taizé," juxtaposing them with the order of the Brothers of Taizé. But Taizé does not have a "second order" (with the brothers being the first). While this distinction is important to retain the significance of the brothers' order in the history of Western monasticism, it's even more important for the sisters, as they have taken vows to communities outside of Taizé. Although there are often several groups of sisters working alongside the brothers, the most notable one hails from an international Catholic order based in Belgium.

The Sisters of St. Andrew are a medieval order dating back almost eight hundred years. Their home base is in Tournai, Belgium, from which they support dozens of satellite groups of sisters ministering in various capacities around the world. Noted for their connection to the mystical spirituality of St. Ignatius of Loyola and their emphasis on taking their ministry beyond the doors of their local milieu, the sisters were an ideal complement to the spiritual life in Taizé.

How the Sisters of St. Andrew first arrived in Taizé is somewhat open to debate. Some believe that it was the sisters who first approached Brother Roger with an offer to help with the welcome and female permanents, but others maintain that Brother Roger invoked their help. The latter is more likely true, according to several brothers. As the story goes, in the early 1960s, Brother Roger was unsure how to minister to the female permanents and pilgrims in a closer context. Several of the Sisters of St. Andrew had already visited Taizé for personal reasons, so in 1966 Brother Roger asked the mother of the community to consider Taizé as a location for their work. Intrigued by the invitation, she sent a couple sisters on a yearly provisional basis. Although the first sisters lived in El Abiodh, soon thereafter a house was found in Ameugny (a neighboring village about a half-mile from the Church of Reconciliation), and the sisters sanctioned Taizé as a permanent place for their ministry. Since 1966, the sisters have offered the community the opportunity to minister to an ever-increasing number of female permanents and young women who wish to spend a week in silence.

Many years later, as the number of Eastern European young people grew, a small group of Polish Ursuline Sisters also settled in the community. The number of Ursuline Sisters depends on the time of year and the various needs of the community. While the Ursuline Sisters are stationed in Taizé, they live in El Abiodh. In addition to the Sisters of St. Andrew and the Ursuline Sisters, many other groups of sisters have assisted at Taizé over the years. These two, however, have been the most enduring.

The relationship between the Brothers of Taizé and the sisters is one of amiable utility. One of the brothers performs the Mass for the sisters on a regular basis, and if requested, a brother will teach a Bible study for them. But the sisters teach Bible Introductions for the adults and offer spiritual guidance for many pilgrims. Although the brothers and sisters work side by side in welcoming pilgrims and organizing housing, the female permanents are almost entirely under the guidance of the sisters. Saying that the brothers have come to rely on the sisters' help in the community is an understatement. Much like the permanents, the sisters' contribution to the larger Taizé community is indispensable. It's safe to say that if it wasn't for this second section of the community it would be difficult—if not impossible— to welcome all the visitors. In short, with the help of the permanents and the sisters, the Brothers of Taizé are able to show hospitality to the third and largest section of the people on the hill: les Jeunes.

LES JEUNES

During an interview I asked one of the brothers, "What do you call the people who visit Taizé? Pilgrims? Visitors? Guests?" Through a chuckle he responded, "We call them 'les Jeunes,'" which literally means "the young" in French. While they recognize that not all the pilgrims coming to Taizé are young, some brothers use this title as a catchall phrase to refer to anyone who does not live in the community.

The brothers may occasionally refer to the pilgrims as visitors, but they rarely refer to them as guests. This connotation is completely contrary to the communal spirit of Taizé. The brothers are not playing host to guests, but attempting to show hospitality to weary sojourners. It is important to understand that the brothers see those who visit Taizé as participants in the community life, even if it's only for the week. If the pilgrims were guests, they wouldn't be asked to share the responsibilities of daily life. The communally shared work is part of what makes Taizé a living example of the gospel. Whether there are one hundred pilgrims visiting in the dead of winter or six thousand in the summer, everyone pulls their weight in the community. Furthermore, everyone is expected to come together to pray three times a day. While a visitor *could* skip a prayer time, the hope is that every participant in the community would gather under one roof and collectively seek after God.

Although "the young" only come to Taizé for a week at a time, they are considered an essential part of what makes Taizé what it is. Arguably, between the nationalities, languages, religious traditions and varying ages, the motley crew assembled in Taizé each year is among the most diverse ecumenical gatherings in the world. Though young and old both come, the young dominate most weeks of the year. By many accounts, the young people were the impetus behind the community's need for adaptation and provision throughout its years.

When asked how the brothers define "young people," their answer traditionally was sixteen to twenty-nine years of age, whereas in recent years, they've begun to consider the growing effects of ex-

El Abiodh

Les jeunes at work

tended adolescence that seems to be developing in our Western culture. Consequently, the brothers have recognized that pilgrims twenty-five to thirty-five years of age might very well qualify as an entirely legitimate demographic of young people. Nonetheless, at this time the brothers still start the "adult" age bracket at thirty, although there are twenty-five- to thirty-five-year-old groups for the Bible Introductions when appropriate.

For those who are over thirty and considering a pilgrimage to Taizé, it's worth being aware of the differences in how the "adult" section of the visitors operates. During the less busy months (October through April), adults and young people intermingle with one another in all parts of Taizé's communal life. Adults who visit Taizé during the busier months, however, encounter a slightly different experience. For example, adults eat, sleep, work and have Bible Introductions in a different part of the grounds. On my first visit to Taizé, I was not aware of this distinction. When the young person who was welcoming me showed me where I would eat and sleep, I felt like an outcast. "You . . . will be sleeping out here," she said, circling an area on the outskirts of the community. "You will eat here [pointing to the adjacent eating area]. And you will only join the young people for prayers." Although I'm sure she meant well, I felt quite rejected at that moment. What I heard was, "You're too old, and I'm going to put you in the leper colony on the outskirts of the community. Don't talk to anyone who looks younger than you."

But through dozens of conversations with adult pilgrims during the trip, I soon realized why the brothers decided to separate the adults and the young people. The more adults I spoke with, the more I realized how many of them came to Taizé when they were young. The stories of the "golden days" of Taizé were more than plentiful. They'd recall: "When I was here when I was twenty-one . . ." or, "Before the church had the orange sails, I was . . ." What was remarkable about these stories was that they offered me a glimpse of Taizé through the years, and they demonstrated to me how significant the community was for the spiritual formation of so many adults. The brothers limit the adults each week and separate them into a different part of the community not because they don't want them there, but because they want to insure that there is space for as many young people as God leads to them. If the brothers opened the community for an unlimited number of adults, it would be saturated by thirty- and fortysomethings.

As one brother put it, "There aren't a lot of places in Europe for young people to go to experience God." Retreat centers, other monasteries and churches are often not very welcoming toward young people. Brother Roger always spoke of the importance of trying to understand young people's search for God. It was important to Brother Roger, however, that both adults and children be present in Taizé. The brothers lined the walls of the church with simple benches to help those who have trouble sitting on the floor. Likewise, during the prayers, the children were invited to sit with Brother Roger, a practice that Brother Alois still continues today. There are even special weeks during the summer where families can gather in Ameugny (the neighboring village where the sisters live) in a house called Olinda. For these weeks, special Bible Introductions are offered at Olinda for the children while their parents attend another. When looked at a little more broadly, it is clear that the Taizé brothers take seriously the role of intergenerational ministry, despite the fact that their focus is bent toward young people.

This openness toward the youth is evident in the communal life and in the demographics of the pilgrims. Since the 1950s, it was the presence of young people that compelled the brothers to consider how they welcomed the visitors. In the 1960s, it was the young people who helped the brothers build their church. In the 1970s, it was the young peoples' desire to gather in Taizé that prompted the brothers to tear down the back wall of the church. Since that time, which also birthed the Council of Youth and Brother Roger's letters, the brothers have carried a torch for the young people of our world. As I said before, the brothers never operated on a "build it and they will come" mentality; rather, the young people came and the brothers had to answer the question "Now what?"

Although it might be considered peculiar by some to say that the young people were the lifeblood of the community, in many ways that's exactly what they are. If the brothers are the heart and mind, and the sisters and permanents are the muscle, it would have to be the young people who give this community its vibrancy for life and its raw and earnest pursuit of holiness. They give it a certain authenticity that is impossible to replicate. No doubt, the brothers are a testimony to what God can do in a group of committed individuals, but the communal life that the young people bring to Taizé is unprecedented. Most Christian organizations would give anything to have the captive audience that Taizé draws each year. But the brothers don't seek to capitalize on this audience. They don't tell the young people to "bring a friend next time." They merely welcome them, accept them for who they are—regardless of their background or ecclesial baggage—and invite them into a holy place to seek after a transcendent God who wants nothing more than to reconcile his creation to himself. It is through the collective prayers of all the different groups in Taizé being lifted up together that we truly see a glimpse of the coming kingdom. Ultimately, what we find in Taizé is a living testimony and a foreshadowing of our future together with God.

8

The Prayers of Taizé

Laudate Dominum, laudate Dominum, omnes gentes, alleluia!
(Sing praise and bless the Lord, peoples! Nations! Alleluia!)

When I sat down to write this chapter, I was having some difficulty writing the first sentence (one of those writer's block things). So, I did what any rational person would do. I asked my six-year-old son how he would open a chapter that's about the prayers of Taizé. His response was, "I like the Alleluias . . . they're nice to sing." I simply replied, "Thanks buddy. I like them too." As I stared at my laptop for another endless few minutes, the innocence and honesty of Judah's answer bounced around my weary mind and ultimately proved far more insightful than I initially realized. I began to wonder if the reason why Judah thinks the Alleluias are "nice to sing" is that they are simple enough that he's able to sing them. The Alleluias and most of the other chants aren't cluttered with complex concepts, wordy phrasing, and awkward and complicated melodies—all characteristics of many of the hymns I grew up with. The chants are simple. Any child can learn one in a matter of minutes. As I thought more about it, I had to ask myself, *Is this why the prayers of Taizé are so appealing to such diverse people groups across our world?* Perhaps it is. Maybe one of the primary reasons the prayers have become so influential across the world is that in their simplicity they're quite possibly the first Christian prayer practice that truly spans the various generations, nationalities and Christian traditions.

What's the equation? Simmered down to the most basic formulation: simple words and a simple melody. In the prayers of Taizé, we find simple biblically based words that seek to unify all traditions of the Christian faith in assorted languages, so as to encompass the diversity of those singing the prayers, and a sophisticated, yet effortless melody that invites even the youngest of pilgrims to lift their voices. Judah was right—the prayers *are* nice to sing; when sung, these simple chants tend to strike a chord deep within our souls that cry out to God.

The prayers of the Taizé community, however, haven't always appealed to such a broad audience. In fact, if we were able to witness the prayers of the community during the 1950s and 1960s, they would be almost unrecognizable to most. The prayers that Christians have come to associate with the Taizé community didn't even exist until the mid 1970s.

Moreover, the repetitious nature of their chants emerged not to attract more pilgrims but to include the ones who were already coming; the brothers were faced with the challenge of how to allow the thousands of young pilgrims to all participate in the daily prayers of the brothers' small community. So, while the brothers did develop the prayers, it was the larger pilgrim community that provided the impetus for their composition. Once again, Brother Roger's desire to live provisionally proved instrumental far beyond his imagination. Rather ironic, don't you think? In North America, we develop, change, and adapt our programs and worship styles with the hope of drawing more bodies into our churches, whereas the brothers developed, changed and adapted their worship style to accommodate and include the masses in their established monastic prayers.

In this chapter we'll look at the story of how the prayers of the Taizé community developed, from Brother Roger's first prayers in an upper room of his house to the beautifully sung chants of six thousand pilgrims on the hill.

THE EARLY PRAYERS

When Brother Roger first moved to Taizé, he prayed by himself three times a day, so as not to impose his faith on those who were using his home as a refuge. When not praying in the little makeshift chapel he created on the top floor of his home, he found solitude in a nearby wood and on occasion in the Romanesque village church. While he was forced to remain in his family's flat in Switzerland because of the Gestapo raiding his house in France, Brother Roger continued in the daily office of prayer with the first three brothers, first in Switzerland and then in their new life together back in Taizé. As more brothers joined the community, the prayers moved from the upper-room chapel to the village church.

In the early 1950s, Brother Roger directed the community's prayers to a more formal monastic liturgy, drawing music from the French Huguenot tradition and the sung *Genevan Psalter.*[1] Father Joseph Gelineau, a French composer and Jesuit priest, contributed heavily to the community's early liturgy, with particular influence on the responsorial Psalms. This liturgy, which was entirely in French, followed a basic pattern: introductory hymns of praise, Scripture, response to Scripture, silence, intercession, Eucharist, closing hymns of praise. Outside of the Scripture reading, the period of silence and the consecration of the Eucharist, the entire liturgy was sung. This basic structure formed the basis of the brothers' daily prayers. Interestingly enough, the structure, although simplified, can still be seen in the liturgy of the Taizé community today.

Very early on, Brother Roger felt that as the community of brothers diversified, so too should the character of their prayers. Even though it was expected that new brothers would learn French in order to participate in the prayers, Brother Roger still wanted the liturgy to reflect the multicultural nature of their growing community. Moreover, it was evident to the brothers that their prior greatly appreciated the vast treasures of music found in other traditions. Thus, by the late 1950s the brothers had already translated several German hymns into French and integrated them into the daily prayers. Likewise, music from Eastern Orthodoxy occasionally supplemented their French liturgy.

Even though the brothers integrated music from other traditions, the language of the liturgy remained in French. This was the case even when the first young pilgrims who joined them were from non-French-speaking countries. As the number of young people increased in the early 1960s, however, so did the concern of the brothers as to how they might include these pilgrims in their worship. The brothers found themselves in a quandary: should they retain the integrity, tradition and historicity of their liturgy or endeavor a means to integrate their visitors? Their answer didn't surface overnight; instead, over the years they adapted the prayers little by little.

THE BIRTH OF THE CHANTS OF TAIZÉ

In the late 1960s, after the first intentional youth gathering, the brothers realized that something would have to change. The planning for the Council of Youth brought about a surge of young people that was unprecedented in the history of the community. Despite the fact that these young people could not speak any French, they tried to follow the liturgy and join in the prayers. In seeking to include the pilgrims, the brothers began reading the Scriptures in other languages, and some of Brother Roger's blessings were in German. Around this time Brother Roger noticed that the young people were lingering in the church after the evening prayers, essentially creating an evening "prayer vigil." He felt that they must remain in solidarity with the young people after the prayers—but what could they sing together? A decision was made to find a more inclusive way of integrating other languages into the liturgy.

The brothers' first attempt was to use common songs from the liturgical repertoire of other countries. This quickly proved limiting, as the pilgrims were quite diverse. While one group of young people was able to sing an imported hymn, others were left only listening. This wasn't sufficient for the brothers. They wanted a solution that would allow everyone to participate in the prayers. Brother Roger felt that no one should have to be a spectator in Taizé. After all, Taizé began as a community of brothers who gathered for common prayer. If the prayers could not include the visiting pilgrims, then the prayers ceased to be the expression of the present-day kingdom of God.

In 1974, with thirty thousand young people congregating in Taizé for the opening of the Council of Youth, Brother Roger felt a disappointment that overshadowed his pleasure at the gathering. As far as he was concerned, if thirty thousand young people were unable pray together, then the Council of Youth did not achieve its intended aim. Brother Roger was always concerned about the youth and about how they experienced the prayers in Taizé. One of the brothers reminisced, "He could put himself in other people's shoes. . . . He understood what it was like for a young person to enter the church for the first time. Brother Roger sought to make Christ's love and compassion immediately accessible. He had the ability to say, 'If I were a young person, I could not understand what was going on here.'" Ultimately, Brother Roger's ability to empathize with the young people influenced how the prayers would change. He knew the answer was in the liturgy but was perplexed as to how they might adapt it for the pilgrims and still remain faithful to the tradition in which the brothers took their vows. One brother was commissioned with the sole task of finding a way to adapt the prayers so that all the young pilgrims could participate.

The brother assigned to the task heard about a "canon form" that was used at the Benedictine monastery built on the side of Montserrat Mountain, in the Catalan region outside of Barcelona.[2] These simple canons were apparently used for centuries to welcome the diverse entourage of pilgrims to the mountain's top and into the Benedictine abbey. The idea of a canon that wasn't in any particular national language was appealing because it offered a universal appeal to all weary sojourners. This mixture of universality and simplicity in a repetitively sung prayer had great resonance in the monastic tradition, and also seemed to promise a certain accessibility for pilgrims of different nations.

Thus on Easter of 1974 the brothers introduced "Cantate Domino" into the liturgy of Taizé, with "Ubi Caritas" following two years later. The welcome reception to this canon led to the integration of more Latin chants. Songs like "Magnificat," "Misericordias Domini" and "Jubilate Deo" soon followed. Some of these chants were borrowed from other nations. For example, in the seventeenth century, a German composer named Michael Praetorius composed "Jubilate Deo," so many of the German pilgrims were familiar with it. It was simple to learn and is still sung in the community today. The brothers felt they had discovered a form that might be helpful, but they had no idea what was to come.

The same year "Ubi Caritas" was introduced in the Easter prayers, Brother Roger took a few brothers and some youth to India to work with Mother Teresa. When they returned to Taizé, a young Indian man named Paul Joseph joined them. One night during his stay, after the evening prayers, Brother Roger, Paul and several brothers remained with the lingering young people for the prayer vigil. They all began singing "Ubi Caritas." The sung prayer was repeated over and over and over again. One of the brothers recalled, "It was a little surprising, because the song went on for twenty minutes . . . because there was so little available to sing." With only three or four simple chants to draw from, Brother Roger made them stretch by singing them over and over again. Although their repertoire was small, Brother Roger "turned it into something more." The provisional nature of the prayer vigil necessitated that they use what they had available, and out of this provision, Brother Roger realized there was something significant about the extended repetition of the chants. While the brothers understood his vision, at times even they wondered about the length of the repetition, which could last as long as twenty minutes per chant. One brother commented, "It was nice, but sometimes it was a lot."

As the brothers' repertoire expanded, however, the length of the repetitions decreased. Before long, they knew that they had discovered something momentous in these sung prayers with simple unifying words, in a universal language repeated again and again. Brother Roger was delighted. It was contemporary, yet connected to the monastic chants of a past era. The path forward became clear—the community needed more chants.

This task was entrusted to Jacques Berthier, an old friend of the brothers who had composed some music for the community twenty years prior. An accomplished composer and musician, Berthier was the organist at the Saint Ignace (Ignatius), a Jesuit church located in Paris. On the surface, his task might have seemed simple—creating one or two lined chants to be sung with an easy melody—but the brothers needed each prayer to reflect the ecumenical nature of the community. So the process began. First the words for the prayers were written with simple rhythms. The aim was to have each prayer directed toward God. Furthermore, the brothers wanted to make sure that the chants were based in Scripture. Consequently, over 90 percent of the Taizé chants are biblically based, with the others being drawn from the creeds of the church. Once the words of each chant were agreed upon, the music was added. They wanted the music to highlight the more salient parts of each prayer.

Berthier would send the brothers his first drafts and the brothers would send them back with suggestions. Some of the chants were too slow; some were too fast. Sometimes the words of the prayers didn't seem right, or the melody was too complicated. Some of the original attempts even fell by the wayside. In fact, many of the final versions of the chants were completely unrecognizable from their first drafts. Through this constant give and take, however, the brothers and Berthier assembled a small but masterful repertoire of chants. By 1978, the community had enough chants to make a recording of the music during one of its European meetings with young people in the Notre Dame cathedral in Paris. Despite his numerous other accomplishments in musical composition, Berthier's legacy will forever include the simple, yet musically sophisticated chants he wrote for the Taizé community.

The brothers finally had enough chants to diversify the evening prayer vigil. By 1978, the community essentially had two parts to the evening prayers: the French liturgy and the vigil of chants, with the latter lasting anywhere between thirty minutes and one-and-a-half hours. For several years after, the community continued to have two parts to the evening prayers.

Then in the early 1980s, Brother Roger wanted to find a way to integrate the two parts so that the pilgrims could more fully participate in the liturgical prayers of the community. This transition, like discovering and developing the chants, didn't happen overnight. For Brother Roger, the question that directed this process was, "What will help the community pray together?" This guiding principle didn't come without a price, however. The monastic liturgy was very beautiful, so there were those in the community who lamented this integration. Furthermore, there was a question of balance. Finding the right mix between using the chants in place of other elements in the French liturgy was not an easy task. Nonetheless, by the mid to late 1980s, the new chants were substituted for much of the monastic liturgy.

Although it may appear today that the chants have completely replaced the old monastic liturgy, they haven't. The structure of the prayers still takes the form of the old liturgy, and several components have remained virtually untouched. It would be more accurate to say that the liturgy was simplified and made more accessible. When considering this transformation from a broader vantage point, it's really quite amazing that the brothers substituted what was sacred to them for what was accessible to all. Yet again, we can see the brothers' relentless commitment to live life provisionally.

Over the years, more songs were composed—even beyond what was originally intended. New chants were written in other languages to encourage diversity in the collective voice of the pilgrims. By the late 1980s, the simple chants were a staple in the spiritual life of the community, and what we now associate with Taizé prayers was the norm. In fact, like many other things, over the last decade of Brother Roger's life the format for the prayers remained essentially untouched.

THE PRAYERS TODAY

Although the prayers went through considerable change, it is still possible to see the liturgy of an era long ago in the prayers today, as they follow an almost dentical liturgical pattern, with only subtle differences: introductory praise, scripture reading, response, silence, intercession, Eucharist (in the morning prayers), closing hymn of praise. This simple rubric has guided the brothers' prayers for almost six decades. A closer look at the prayers reveals the thought, consideration and intentionality that the brothers have invested in the liturgy.

Introductory praise. As the gong of the bells dissolves into silence, the pilgrims wait for a brother who functions as the opening cantor for the particular prayer time to usher the church into the prayers. After a brother sings he opening measure of the first chant, the entire community joins in. Often he first chant is an "Alleluia" through which a cantor offers up sung adoration to God in between the voices of the assembly. Depending on the time of day, his part of the liturgy might contain two or three chants. For example, after an opening "Alleluia," "Laudate Omnes Gentes" might be sung.

Laudate Dominum, laudate Dominum, omnes gentes, alleluia!
(Sing, praise and bless the Lord. Sing, praise and bless the Lord.
Peoples! Nations! Alleluia!)

The morning and evening prayers can last up to an hour, but the shorter midday prayers only have time for one or two opening chants. Selecting these introductory praise chants is a challenge for the brothers, as there are a number of variables that have to be considered. In the morning, for example, chants with lower keys are selected, as most pilgrims are still waking up. These first songs are viewed as a way to ease people into the morning prayers. For the afternoon prayers, the brothers attempt to select songs with a joyful tone and tempo; with long days and short nights in Taizé, noontime prayers are often more of a challenge for those in need of additional rest (brothers notwithstanding). Typically, the evening prayers also feature a more joyful repertoire of chants and are personified by an anticipatory feeling from the onset of the first hymn of praise. Each subsequent chant moves the pilgrims toward a contemplative mindset, in preparation for the reading of the Scripture.

In addition to daily variants, the different times of the year also bring alterations to the introductory chants. In the less busy winter months, when there are only a few hundred pilgrims, the brothers tend to use a canon from the Psalter and alternate singing between the verses. During the busier months, however, they use one soloist and a refrain in which all can participate. As I mentioned earlier, introductory praise was my son's favorite part. The ease with which he was able to participate, even at a young age, is part of what makes this opening chant so welcoming and accessible for all.

Scripture reading. After the whole community sings two or three chants of praise, one of the brothers approaches a lectern in the back of the brothers' hedge-lined area. The lectern, which is visible from almost everywhere in the church, becomes the visual center for this part of the prayers, as everyone turns and faces it. The Scripture reading is one of the only times during the prayers when the whole assembly sits toward the center facing one another. During that moment, the rustle of bodies, prayer stools and loose papers floods the church as everyone settles in with anticipation for the reading of the Word.

Amplified through a microphone, the brother's voice rings through the church as he reads a passage of Scripture aloud. The passage is most commonly read in English, French or German, although occasionally another language is employed depending on the various nationalities of the pilgrim community that particular week. In the busier months, the brother will read the passage in two different languages to accommodate the diversity in the church.

During the morning and evening prayers, the brothers read the Scripture from the lectern, but in the shorter midday prayers the reading is done by one of the brothers in the center of the assembly floor to save the time it takes people to shift positions. Through each reading, the brothers follow a lectionary calendar that enables them to make it through the Bible in two years. When the pilgrims number over a thousand, however, the readings often take a slight detour. Because many of the visitors in Taizé are just starting their spiritual journeys, Brother Roger always thought it was in their best interest that the most fundamental aspects of the gospel be read. Furthermore, with the ecumenical nature of the community in mind, the brothers tend to focus on unifying passages. The strength in this approach is that those gathered in the church are drawn together in the readings. The disadvantage is that the same passages get repeated a lot during the summer months. The brothers try to combat this repetition by reading the passages in different languages, as they believe it's always refreshing to hear the Word of God in other tongues.

When the lectionary passages are used, the particular verses that the brothers read are also carefully chosen in light of those visiting Taizé. The brothers try to read only the core of each passage, as they believe it's better for people to focus on a certain amount of the Scripture at one time. If the reading carries on for two or three minutes, the brothers feel that the pilgrims' minds will wander too far from the essential aspects in each passage. Reading a shorter selection allows the pilgrims to listen and meditate on the words. Mystics in the medieval period had a practice of reading a little Scripture, but really ingesting it. Likewise, the brothers desire for the pilgrims to chew on the text, to taste what it's saying. They believe rumination is not an intellectual endeavor but one of the heart. By only reading short, essential passages, the brothers allow young people to ponder the significance of the Scripture for their own lives.

This practice of reading shorter passages of Scripture and meditating on them is somewhat foreign in our capitalistic culture. Many churchgoers today come to church with a business mindset that says, "Give me the information, and tell me why I want to know this and what I should do with it." It's an intellectual commodity that often fails to authentically transform the hearers of the Word. In Taizé, however, the reading of Scripture is revered. The movement of the assembly toward the lectern is an act of focusing their attention on God's words through the testimony of the Holy Canon. In the time of Scripture reading, the brothers want the short passages they've chosen to genuinely allow the Holy Spirit to speak to each individual.

This hasn't always been the philosophy behind the readings for the brothers. In the 1970s, for example, there were two longer readings, much like what is found in many of our mainline churches in North America today. As the brothers adapted the sung prayers, though, the Scripture reading was also evaluated. It was determined that if the goal was for people to digest the Word of God, they must be fed appropriate doses. As one brother put it, "It's that the Word can stay in us when we turn it over and over and find life in it."

The heart of what the brothers hope to see happen in the reading is that the young people would gather the sense of the passage and that they would encounter the heart of the gospel. This might come through hearing the whole of the read passage, but it might also come through a particular phrase or word. As a brother was describing this for me, it immediately reminded me of *lectio divina. Lectio divina,* which is Latin for "divine reading," is a meditative method of reading that made its first appearance in the works of Origen in the third century. Both St. Augustine and St. Benedict included *lectio divina* as a central practice of monastic life. Although it took many forms throughout the history of the church, its intention remains the same: to invite the listener to genuinely meditate on the words of Scripture.

In the past decade, as Protestants have begun to embrace some of the more contemplative practices of the church, *lectio divina* has made an incredible resurgence. Today one of the most common ways of practicing *lectio divina* involves reading a passage several times with short intervals of silence in between each reading. After each reading, the listeners try to focus on a single word or phrase that stands out to them. The intervals of silence are offered as a time for rumination and meditation to take place. Perhaps the reason *lectio divina* is growing in popularity in the present day is due to the fact that we reserve very little time to simply listen to the words of Scripture. This divine reading forces us to stop, listen and ponder how the Holy Spirit is speaking to us. In short, it allows the words of God to penetrate our souls.

When I pressed one of the brothers on whether or not they were purposefully using a form of *lectio divina* in the prayers, he merely said they were similar in form and intent but not directly drawn from the ancient prayer practice. The same spirit is found in the prayers of Taizé, but the structure is different. While the young people have time to rest quietly in the short text, the intent is not for them to "find" a specific phrase through successive readings. The silence that follows the Scripture reading is less structured. Each person must decide for themselves how they will use it. In any case, the Scripture reading in the prayers at Taizé is an invitation to hear God's voice as revealed to us in Scripture.

Scriptural response. As the assembly turns back toward the front of the church, a response to the Scripture is sung by the whole assembly. The response is often found on an extra piece of paper that is picked up when the pilgrims enter the church, and it's always in French. Interestingly, the Scriptural response is one of the lasting remnants of the old French liturgy that the community used decades ago. Although most pilgrims are unaware of its historical significance, for the community of brothers (in particular the older brothers), the response is an important reminder of an era past and how the provisional nature of the community has brought about dynamic changes. The response is never long but it does stand out, as it offers a segue into one of the most important and unique aspects of the prayers in Taizé: the time of silence.

Silence. One of the most defining aspects of the prayer time in Taizé is the extended period of silence. After the response, the display boxes with the songbook numbers go blank, and the entire church settles into a peaceful silence. For pilgrims who are in Taizé for the first time, the silence can seem like it's never going to end. I experienced this sensation during my first week in the community. When the silence began, it was rather serene to sit in the Church of Reconciliation with nothing but my own meditations, but before long, the question, "How long will this go on?" kept running through my mind.

In a fast-paced, technologically saturated Western milieu, being silent is a rarity, especially in North America, where many of us are bombarded—from the moment our alarm radio wakes us in the morning until the last lingering song on our iPod lulls us to sleep—by a never-ending barrage of auditory stimuli. It's no secret that we Americans are not a nation of silence. The practice of silence probably began crumbling around the time the radio and the television were invented. Now, with the portability and ease of carrying your entire music library in the palm of your hand, we've got a generation of young people whose daily lives are accompanied by a continuous self-selected soundtrack. It's easy to understand why sitting in silence for an extended period might seem like an eternity.

In addition to being novel in our culture, silence can be rather scary for some. The fear is often magnified in religious settings, because there is an underlying assumption that we ought to be engaging in some sort of soul searching in our spiritual lives. Silence is one of those scarcely utilized mediums that ushers us into the holy. While sometimes churches offer short periods of silence during their worship, those periods often seem more cursory than transformative. For example, in my denomination we offer moments of silence for the prayers of confession or silent petition, but rarely do we have extended periods of silence through which we can listen to the still, small voice of God. As a consequence of both these factors—not being used to silence and the fear we may have about it—many American pilgrims become preoccupied during their first few times in the prayers by wondering when the period of silence will end.

How long the silence lasts actually depends on several factors. The duration of the silence can be as short as six or seven minutes (in the midday prayers) and as long as twelve minutes in the morning and evening prayers. It's not a set pattern that determines its length but an intentional decision that requires careful consideration and a prayerful spirit. Before his death Brother Roger decided when the silence was over; then he pressed a little button that signaled to the brother playing the keyboard to begin the next chant. Now the task of ending the period of silence rests in the hands of the new prior, Brother Alois.

Why is silence so central to the prayers at Taizé? To answer this question we must look to the community's foundation. It should come as little surprise that silence was always significant for Brother Roger. Even as a young boy, he spent extended periods alone in the garden in silence. Moreover when Brother Roger contracted tuberculosis as a young man, he walked for ours in the mountain forests, contemplating the nature of life and God. This affinity for silence continued into his twenties. During his time studying theology at the University of Lausanne, Brother Roger had a retreat with Carthusian monks, who live most of their monastic lives in silence. The experience proved so profound for Roger that his father was concerned he would not return to his schooling. Then in the early 1940s, when Taizé was first becoming a place of refuge, Brother Roger took many silent walks in the forest. It was during those times that God strengthened and renewed him for what would come after. Thus, the practice of meditative silence continually defined Brother Roger's spiritual journey throughout his life. It's no wonder that it became such a significant component in the liturgy from the beginning. Because of his emphasis on silence, this part of the liturgy has become a hallmark of the Taizé prayers.

If the silence has become so central to the prayers, what exactly is supposed to be going on during this period? It's safe to say that many pilgrims ask this question as they sit in the stillness of the church. "What am I supposed to be doing right now?" Even when asked later what they do during the silence, many young people are unable to articulate how they use that time. Answers like "being still" and "waiting" were among the most common in my conversations with them. For many, it's a chance to breathe; it's a time carved out to allow pilgrims to *be,* in the most existential meaning of the word. It's not a structured time that requires pilgrims to accomplish this or that, but an opportunity to encounter God. Words and language will always fall short in describing those transcendent moments we have with our Creator when we actually sit and listen.

In retrospect, I too struggled with what I was supposed to be doing during the silence. Should I be praying? Is it bad to look around? Am I meant to contemplate the Scripture that was just read? These questions and many others like them filled my mind. I'm so used to living a life that is full of tasks that need to be accomplished. As a young person, I was taught to actively pray. Adoration, confession, thanksgiving, supplication, intercession, petition and praise were some of the types of prayer that I was expected to employ during my devotional times; words, whether in my head or out loud, were the medium I used to communicate to God.

I realize now that I was either trying to praise God with adoration or ask for something from God through petition or intercession. What I failed to learn how to do was to sit before God and listen and remain in the stillness of the moment and allow God to penetrate my soul. Being task-oriented is contrary to the prayer life in Taizé. The prayers are aimed at creating a space for us to simply be before our King.

With that said, however, an existential encounter is not an expectation of the brothers. In fact, they have no expectations for what actually goes on during the silence. It is precisely this lack of expectation that they feel most characterizes the silence. At the core of it, the brothers hope that pilgrims experience freedom to encounter God or the Scripture in their own ways. Brother Roger never said to the brothers or the young people, "This is what you ought to be doing during the silence." What he did say was ultimately more suggestive than prescriptive. For example, one brother recalled Brother Roger remarking, "There are moments when silence can be everything in prayer." Apparently Brother Roger was also often heard quoting Saint Augustine: "When our lips are closed and our soul is open before God, our heart speaks to God." For Brother Roger, our hearts have their own language that surfaces only when we are silent. Without a doubt the silence is at the heart of the prayers in Taizé.

An analogy might help us understand the importance of the silence even more. If we think of each prayer time as a meal, it helps us frame the various aspects of the liturgy. In a seven-course meal, the first few courses build to the entrée. But we don't rush through the first courses to get to the entrée; instead we savor each course for what it is. Each course, however, builds to a center and then moves from that center to leave the patron with a holistic dining experience. In a similar manner, each part of the liturgy points toward the center—the silence. The silence is the entrée. The Scripture that's read right before the silence is offered to feed our souls, and the silence can function as a point of discovery. It gives us time to ruminate and ponder the simplicity and depth of the passage.

In a way, the silence also operates much like a sermon or homily would in our contemporary worship services. After the Word is read, the pastor usually explains, illustrates and applies the Word to our daily lives. In Taizé, however, there is no explanation for the texts in the prayer times. Rather, the text is allowed to speak for itself. The brothers recognize the living nature of the Scriptures and allow for the text's "self-authenticating" nature to manifest itself in the silence of the pilgrim. While we might be tempted to argue that young people need direction and guidance in understanding the texts, we must also remember that the brothers choose passages that contain the simplest precepts of the faith and offer reconciliation and peace, while still challenging the listeners to live a life of witness. In the end, the silence offers a certain freedom and space to explore, contemplate and discover the mysteries of the faith and our place in it—an opportunity that is often absent in our Western understanding of spirituality.

Intercession. Following this period of silence is a responsive prayer of intercession. The intercession begins with the solo voice of a cantor breaking the silence with the refrain "Kyrie eleison." Even before the brother is finished, the pilgrims join in echoing this ancient cry, "Lord, have mercy." Then the brother sings a prayer of intercession on behalf of those suffering throughout the world. The intercessions are often sung in different languages, allowing different pilgrims to hear the prayer in their native tongue. As each intercession ends, the brother sings "Kyrie eleison," which is the assembly's key to join in the response. This exchange lasts for several minutes, depending on how many prayers of intercession are offered. If "Kyrie eleison" is not used, often an equivalent response in another language is used. Or, despite its significance in the liturgy, the sung intercessions are occasionally replaced by a meditative reading from a prayer by Brother Alois.

Eucharist. What follows the intercession in the morning is perhaps the most distinctive difference between the three daily prayers. In the midday and evening prayers, the intercession is followed by another chant, moving the liturgy toward the end of the prayers. In the morning, however, the Lord's Prayer and the Eucharist follow the intercession. The Lord's Prayer is always sung, sometimes in English, other times in another language more suited to the national makeup of the pilgrims for the week. When the Lord's Prayer is finished, the assembly sings another chant while the Eucharist is distributed.

It should be noted that the Eucharistic elements are not consecrated during the general morning prayers but rather separately, in an early-morning Catholic Mass and a Protestant service each day. Although most pilgrims receive the Eucharist during the morning prayers, some prefer to receive it at these early-morning Eucharistic gatherings. For Catholic pilgrims who wish to receive the Eucharist during the morning prayers, there are brothers stationed around the church distributing the elements. For those from churches belonging to the Reformed tradition, Holy Communion is distributed by young people to the right of the icon of the resurrection near the cross. Occasionally, the Divine Liturgy is celebrated for Orthodox Christians when an Orthodox priest is visiting the community. There are also young permanents stationed in various locations around the church with small baskets containing blessed bread. This offering is for those who do not feel ready to receive the Eucharist, those who aren't baptized, little children or those who for different reasons do not receive Communion.

On Sundays the Catholic Eucharist is offered in the morning prayers. The Protestant Eucharist is available at a Saturday night service and during Sunday morning prayers. When an Orthodox priest is available, the Orthodox Eucharist is offered in an earlier service on Sunday morning. Depending on the time of year, the Protestant and the Orthodox Eucharistic services are either available in the village church or in the Orthodox chapel, next to the crypt in the basement of the Church of Reconciliation.

Closing praise. After the Eucharist in the morning or the intercession in the afternoon and evening, the prayer times are brought to a close through several chants. The number of chants depends on the prayer time. During the morning and evening prayers, two or three songs are sung, whereas in the midday prayers only one or two songs at the most conclude the prayer time. When the last chant has been sung, the prior leads the brothers out of the church. After the morning and afternoon prayers the brothers carry on with their daily tasks, however, after the evening prayers, many remain for the prayer vigil.

Prayer vigil. For many pilgrims the vigil that takes place after the evening prayers is a regular part of their experience at Taizé. Once the brothers leave, many of the young people make their way to Oyak, but hundreds of searching pilgrims still remain in the Church of Reconciliation. The expanse of the assembly floor, usually covered by dense crowds, is visible in between the scattered pilgrims remaining. Brothers place themselves around the church and wait with open ears as young people come to them to share about their spiritual journey. As long as there are voices to be heard, the brothers remain. Not everyone speaks to a brother, though; for some young people, remaining in the church to sing is sufficient.

The prayer vigil typically takes place in Taizé Sunday evenings through Thursday evenings, offering five nights where the young people can extend the evening prayers for deeper searching. The structure really is quite simple. One of the brothers remains to play various chants from the songbook, and because of the lack of an official ending time, pilgrims are often able to experience longer repetitions with the chants, giving the vigil a more contemplative characteristic than the scheduled prayer times.

On Friday nights something significantly different transpires. The evening prayers take place as usual, except that before the brothers leave, two or three will take the icon of the cross that was painted by Brother Eric and place it horizontally on several blocks in the center of the brothers' seating area. Then the brothers gather around the cross in prayer. Some place their foreheads on it while others simply kneel before it. After a few minutes they exit as usual. As they're leaving, several permanents create open gaps in the short artificial hedges that normally separate the brothers from the assembly. Once these openings are ready, young people flow through to the cross like water rushing through a broken dam. One by one, they place their foreheads on the cross in solidarity with Christ. As a young person leaves the cross, another one quickly fills her spot. This process goes on until the very last pilgrim has placed his forehead on the icon of the cross. Although technically this takes place during the evening vigil, this ritual has come to be known as the Prayers around the Cross.

The Prayers around the Cross weren't always a part of the weekly liturgy. In the mid 1970s the brothers noticed that on Good Friday the young people would gather around the cross and pray late into the night. This practice went on for years every Good Friday, until one year the brothers noticed that Russian Christians were praying around the cross on Friday nights. As this pattern continued, the brothers inquired as to its emergence. They learned that these Russian young people were praying at the cross as an act of solidarity and communion with their friends who were in prison. They invited the brothers to join them—and they did.

Shortly thereafter, Brother Roger thought a bit more about this practice and decided that perhaps the community should pray together around the cross every Friday of the year. Hence the practice of the Prayers around the Cross was born. Originally the cross was left upright, but after quite some time, as suddenly as the Prayers around the Cross began, a decision was made that the cross should be horizontal and on the ground. Perhaps they did this to allow pilgrims to surround the cross and touch it, or maybe they were simply concerned it was going to fall. No one is quite sure how the cross ended up on the ground, but it did, and it is placed there every Friday night. Whatever the reason, putting the cross horizontally on the ground offers pilgrims the opportunity to place their foreheads on it—an intimate and ancient symbol of solidarity.

Many pilgrims process to the cross on their knees. They also kneel while they wait to get near the cross and place their foreheads on it. Apparently, in the early 1990s many of the young Polish Christians began processing to the cross this way as an expression of their ecclesial heritage and tradition. Slowly but surely this practice caught on in the Prayers around the Cross and is a relatively common practice today.

Shortly after the community started having the Prayers around the Cross weekly, they realized that they couldn't have Good Friday every week without Easter. Thus, the brothers decided to have an Easter celebration each week as well. Some know it as the Vigil of Lights, others the Festival of Lights, but to many of the brothers, it's simply the Easter vigil. The Vigil of Lights (as I came to know it) is similar to a candlelight service on Christmas Eve. As people enter the church for the Saturday evening prayers, everyone gets a self-extinguishing taper in addition to the songbook. At the end of the evening prayers, the children sitting around Brother Alois (and before him Brother Roger) approach the Christ candle and light their tapers. These children then walk up and down the aisles lighting everyone else's candles. By the time everyone's taper is lit, the church looks like a sea of dancing flames—and six thousand flames illuminating the belly of the church is definitely a sight to behold. The church becomes a living example of reconciliation in the lives of those young people. For the first time in many of their lives, these young people physically see *one* community of faith, together under *one* roof, worshiping the *one* true God.

I believe one of reasons that so many Europeans are drawn to Taizé is that, for many young people who have grown up in the tension of religious traditions, Taizé incarnates their deepest longing for peace. In this community, the age-old Catholic-Protestant polemic is swallowed in an ocean of reconciliation. For the majority of young people who visit, Taizé is the only place in the world where they can worship in communion with all Christian traditions freely. After a week of prayers in Taizé, working alongside young people of other traditions, it's no wonder that many pilgrims are moved to tears during this climactic vigil.

In the end, all can come to Taizé and participate in the prayers. For the past several decades, Christians have relished the beauty of the Taizé chants for obvious reasons. They are beautiful and easy to sing, and they bring a contemplative mood that so many Christians are longing for as a way to escape our hectic lifestyles. I would argue, however, that there is something more to the chants than meets the ears. When we consider the nature of the liturgy's development and the level of intentional adaptation that the brothers have invested into the transformation of their prayers, we have no choice but to stand in awe of what God has birthed in and through the Taizé community. Perhaps for the first time in the history of the church, a manner of praying has emerged that links young and old, Catholics and Protestants, and dozens of different nationalities. Brother Roger and the Brothers of Taizé have given the world a gift, and although they might humbly downplay these accolades, the truth remains that through their obedience to Christ's call and their desire to be a sign of reconciliation on this earth, they have uncovered something that truly brings God's children together.

9

The Heart of Taizé

Nothing can ever come between us and the love of God,
the love of God revealed to us in Christ Jesus.

∅

Brother Roger didn't wake up one day and say, "If we do this and that, I bet tons of young people will come"—yet, tons of young people is exactly what they got. What's their secret? Is it something in the water in Taizé that keeps these young people flocking back to the community in hoards? Why do so many young people travel so far to spend a week in a community of brothers who pray three times a day, offer several hours of Bible study and sharing groups, and ask the young people to participate in work around the grounds?

North Americans practically bribe young people to come to our churches. We lower the bar of expectations in hopes that our young people will grace us with their mere bodily presence in our dank basements and remodeled youth rooms. The brothers give them jobs like cleaning toilets and cooking meals and we give them foosball tables, ping pong and second-hand sofas. The brothers invite them to join in three prayer times, a Bible Introduction and sharing groups for almost five hours of direct spiritual engagement, whereas we often just hope they won't leave early and miss out on our songs and five-minute talk about a radical hippie named Jesus. The whole thing seems counterintuitive. As one brother put it, the mystery of why young people come to Taizé is the "million dollar question" that everyone asks.

If church leaders around the world could figure out the key to Taizé's apparent success with young people, it would be processed, packaged and available for purchase faster than you could find Taizé on a map (which is more difficult than you might think). In fact, for the past few decades, many Christian leaders, pastors, scholars and students have traveled to Taizé with the hope of "uncovering" their secret for reaching young people.

When I first decided to research the community, I too was under the anticipation that I could crack the code. Once in Taizé, however, I realized there is no secret code and thus nothing really to crack, per se. What I did find was a real community of brothers who are an authentic and living example of Christ's reconciliation in the world. While I wasn't aware of it at first, as my research continued I became more confident that the appeal of Taizé isn't some "thing" that could be exported or imported, but rather theological threads which are woven into the fabric of the community. The more I considered these themes in light of my own ecclesial context, I surmised that, if conceptualized properly, these themes could be fostered and cultivated in other Christian communities and churches.

I believe the three prominent theological themes of Taizé are *reconciliation, freedom* and *trust*. On the surface, these might seem commonplace for a church or religious organization. In Taizé, though, they are at the center of life in a way that is unthinkable to many churches around the globe. I believe there is a lot we can learn from how the brothers foster these themes in Taizé. When we truly consider reconciliation, freedom and trust in light of our own local church body, we have to ask ourselves if they're truly at the center of our life together or if they remain on the periphery of our church life, only to be pondered by the theologically inquisitive. As I delve into how these themes are woven into Taizé's communal life, I invite you to consider the need for these three themes in the life and liturgy of your own worshiping community.

Before I plumb the depths of the three themes, however, I must offer you a few preliminary remarks concerning the contents of this chapter. First, the "themes" which I am about to expound are based on the conclusions of my own research. While the Brothers of Taizé have supported my writing this book from the onset, in no way do I claim to have unearthed the hidden "secret of Taizé." In fact, it's quite the opposite. Only through countless hours poring over my research and reflecting on the community have I realized that there is no secret to their "success," as I mentioned before.

Moreover, there is no "Taizé theology" that can be ascribed to the community as a whole, an issue that Brother Roger was rather adamant about. He never wanted one theology or a single perspective to drive the life and worship of this collective community, in part because every brother comes from a different tradition. None of them was required to break ties with their ecclesial traditions to become a brother of Taizé; rather the various Christian traditions of each brother are celebrated in their unified fellowship. In this way, each brother learns about another brother's doctrinal emphases and distinctions. If the Brothers of Taizé attempted to align themselves with a particular tradition of Christianity or create a new denomination of the faith, it would only set them against the most significant aspect of the community: reconciliation. The acceptance of another Christian's ecclesial tradition is at the core of what fosters true understanding and forgiveness. Acceptance is what makes reconciliation in Christ possible. Thus, with my caveats stated, that's where we'll begin: with the reconciliation that is so essential to the community of Taizé.

RECONCILIATION AND ACCEPTANCE

From the moment Brother Roger first set foot in the little village of Taizé, reconciliation permeated his thoughts and actions. He believed we could not truly love Christ without also loving our neighbor, and he concretely demonstrated both his love for Christ and others by living among the poor and offering hospitality to war refugees. As the community developed and new brothers joined Brother Roger, it became apparent that genuine ecumenism would be one of the most significant challenges the community would face. After all, for over four hundred years estrangement had existed between Protestants and Catholics. But for the young Swiss theologian, it was four hundred years too many. Brother Roger understood all of humanity to be reconciled to God in and through Christ. Thus, if we are all reconciled to Christ and accepted by God through his work, our love for Christ must also extend to others by accepting them. For Brother Roger, this was never truer than in our relationships with other Christians. After all, how can the world see Christ's reconciliation when his bride is divided into opposing traditions?

Our differences dissipate when we recognize that Christ is the link in our kinship with other Christians. Christ's death on the cross procured our reconciliation with our Father in heaven. We are no longer estranged from our Creator. When Christ ascended he promised us the Holy Spirit, who would enable us to incarnate Christ's reconciliation to the world. When we claim Christ's identity as our own, therefore, we also accept the calling to become bearers of reconciliation. For the brothers, this begins with the loving acceptance of our neighbor, because both we and our neighbor are accepted by Christ.

In other words, Christ ought to become the central and primary connecting point between all of humanity. When he's our point of union, we are free to accept our calling to love one another, because Christ has already accepted us. At Taizé, this sentiment is felt in a very pronounced way. Young people are accepted into the life of the community and into the prayers without consideration for their ecclesial tradition, nationality or economic status. In this authentic expression of acceptance, all are equal in Taizé; the community becomes a living example of reconciliation.

This, to a large degree, is why the Taizé chants were birthed—to help bring young people from different Christian traditions together in a unified expression of prayer. At Taizé, the traditional barriers are broken down and Christ-centered solidarity is erected in its stead. Brother Alois believes when Christians are truly ready to give their whole lives to the heart of the gospel, the undivided church will emerge. This doesn't mean that we must break ties with our ecclesial heritage. We should, however, recognize that it will cost us something. True acceptance of our neighbor forces us to put aside our own pride and ideologies and focus on what is central to all Christians.

According to Oliver Clement, a theologian and highly respected friend of the community, reconciliation can only surface by acknowledging what is not essential. In accepting others, we aren't ignoring our differences but instead we're focusing on those aspects that unify us. In the words of the prominent German pastor and theologian Dietrich Bonhoeffer: "The more genuine and deeper our community becomes, the more will everything else between us recede, the more clearly and purely will Jesus Christ and his work become the one and only thing that is vital between us."[1]

One of the ways the Brothers of Taizé foster reconciliation stems from their spirit of hospitality. In *The Rule,* Brother Roger wrote, "It is Christ himself whom we receive in a guest. Let us learn to welcome."[2] While there are "official" brothers who have taken vows to the monastic life in Taizé, they freely welcome pilgrims as fellow siblings in Christ. This kinship personifies a spirit of acceptance and runs amply throughout the pilgrim's stay. Being received as a part of this kinship is significant for drawing young people to this community.

Gael, a French twentysomething from the coastal province of Brittany, told me the reason he continued to come to Taizé was that no matter what had gone wrong in his life the previous year, he was always accepted and welcomed back. During an informal interview with two girls, ages fifteen and sixteen, "welcomed" and "accepted" were their first responses to the question, "What was your first impression of Taizé on the day that you arrived?" They shared with me that despite the vast differences in the young people that week, they experienced an unexpected unity. For the first time in their lives, they could worship alongside Roman Catholics and Orthodox believers. Youth who had not been in Taizé long immediately picked up on the critical importance of Christian acceptance there. The differences in traditions and backgrounds that the young people brought with them quickly became irrelevant in their budding relationships with one another. Bonhoeffer writes that the "exclusion of the weak and insignificant, the seemingly useless people, from a Christian community may actually mean the exclusion of Christ; in the poor [person] Christ is knocking at the door."[3]

When I asked one of the brothers why he thought young people were drawn to Taizé, without hesitation he stated, "They feel accepted." For the brothers, this acceptance is a necessary part of obeying the second greatest commandment; "Jesus makes his disciples a part of his own way of life; he enables them to love as he loves."[4] In Taizé, young people take part in a qualitatively new way of life in both giving and receiving loving acceptance.

CONTEXTUAL RECONCILIATION

Observing this powerful acceptance in Taizé throughout my research has necessarily caused me to continually ask, "But what does reconciliation look like for my own social and spiritual milieu?"

When I asked Brother Alois what reconciliation might look like in another context, he offered me an example from 1992, when the brothers brought their message of reconciliation to the midsized city of Dayton on the southwest side of Ohio. For three months, the brother prepared for the gathering. As part of this preparation, the brothers held weekly prayers for the community in which the meeting would take place. They'd realized during their search for a host city that Dayton was divided by the Miami River. This geographic division was even more pronounced by the ethnic division that existed as well. On one side of the river a predominately Caucasian community existed, and on the other side, an African American community. This troubled the brothers. How could they bring reconciliation to a city that was divided both geographically and ethnically by a single river?

A decision was made to have the weekly prayers on alternating sides of the river. Each week, Christians from one side had to cross a bridge to join in a common worship time. I could see in Brother Alois's face as he told me the story that true reconciliation transpired during those months in Dayton. The symbolism as well as the spirit of worship that emerged from these common times of prayer was a testimony to Christ's acceptance of us. For the first time in many of their lives, these Ohioans were able to openly accept one another with Christ's love—which points once again to the truth of the brothers' belief that one of the keys to reconciliation lies in our ability to accept one another.

When I first started my research in Taizé, I often asked young people why they came to the community. The feeling of being accepted was abundantly present in almost all of my interviews. Again and again, young people echoed the sentiment that they felt accepted in Taizé. It didn't matter if they were Catholic or Protestant; it didn't matter if they were from an Eastern European or African country; and it didn't matter if they were poor or rich. For the first time in many of these young peoples' lives, they felt accepted in a religious environment—they *belonged*.

For example, Mano, a twenty-eight-year-old from Italy, has spent a week in Taizé after his summer holiday for the past twelve years. Mano shared with me that in Taizé he felt like he belonged, something that he had not experienced at any church in Italy. While he identified with the tradition of his upbringing, he ultimately felt estranged. For Mano, feeling accepted by God and others comes in the form of a week in Taizé at the end of each summer. In this community, Mano was able to experience reconciliation with God and extend that reconciliation to his neighbor, no matter their background. I've often wondered where he would experience Christ's reconciliation if he hadn't experienced this acceptance in Taizé. Do other young people experience genuine belonging and acceptance in our churches, or like Mano, do they only experience impersonal religion or perhaps even estrangement?

Clearly we can learn from the brothers' emphasis on acceptance and reconciliation, but the question remains, how do we actually usher reconciliation into our own contexts? Better yet, is it possible to cultivate the type of acceptance that has come to characterize the Taizé community? I believe there are three ways we can begin to see this happen in our local congregations. I should warn you, however, that all three require us to take a hard look at ourselves in light of the calling God has placed on our lives.

First we need to look inward and ask ourselves if we really want to share with others the reconciliation we experience through Christ. We live in a culture that prizes equality and diversity on an ideological level, but we seldom see that ideal manifest itself as a reality. Do we really long for diversity in our churches? Our sermons, slick brochures and church websites often display an array of different types of people—young and old, black and white, families and singles—but appearance is not enough. Saying "We value diversity" isn't sufficient if we don't practice Christ-centered acceptance. Are we willing to embrace the gospel's call to care for the poor and the needy? Are we willing to worship among various traditions or ethnic groups? Or is our call for diversity only lip service?

In other words, do we really want to accept others who aren't the same as us? If we do, the heart of reconciliation must begin within. We can't claim to accept all people if in our hearts we haven't genuinely accepted those who are different than we are. Whether it's a racial divide or an ecclesial chasm, we must face the fact that Christ calls us to loving acceptance—which is why this reconciliation must first begin in our own relationship with Christ. Once we view ourselves as accepted before the Father and coheirs with Christ, we then begin to extend that gift to those around us. When Christ made all things new, he restored in us the image of God. Moreover, this image was restored in all of humanity. As a consequence, when we see our neighbor we ought to see the image of God; we ought to see Christ.

As different as some may be, beginning with an understanding of our acceptance before God enables us to accept others because Christ accepted us. A fuller understanding of this aspect of salvation carries with it consequences. It means that we may have to take risks that involve making ourselves vulnerable and open to rejection—risks that Christ willingly accepted on the path to the cross. If we are truly going to see acceptance and reconciliation fostered in our ecclesial environments, we must begin with our own desires for acceptance. If we truly want to bear Christ's message of reconciliation, we must begin by experiencing our own acceptance and then showing that acceptance to others.

Second, we must be willing to not view our own tradition as exclusive but instead accept the fact that God has revealed himself through the various traditions in the history of the Judeo-Christian church. Before entering seminary I was a Protestant youth minister for six years. During that time I served in different churches but was amazed and troubled at all of them by how pejorative some Protestants were toward Roman Catholics. Snide remarks about Catholic theology or doctrine always felt horribly wrong to me. With that said, I'm willing to bet that the same sort of subtle belittling occurs in many Catholic circles toward Protestants as well. In addition to my time as a youth pastor, marrying an Irish Catholic bride made me even more aware of how bifurcated our faith has become. If we really desire to become a sign of reconciliation to the world, we've got some serious family issues to resolve.

Why is it that Christians are so condemning and judgmental of each other? The time is long overdue for Christians to let go of those aspects of our traditions and denominations that divide us and begin focusing on the essential aspects of faith that unite us. I believe one of the reasons over 100,000 pilgrims travel to the community to pray with the brothers each year is because through them we can witness an actual example of the gospel message Christ has called us all to live. All varieties of the Christian faith are welcomed and accepted in Taizé. Can we genuinely say this about our own churches? Are we engaging in fellowship and worship with other Christian traditions on a regular basis? Perhaps before we "evangelize" the world, we ought to take a hard look at how we're loving our own brothers and sisters in Christ. In short, if we don't start taking steps toward reconciliation in the Christian faith, maybe we have no business sharing about God's love.

Finally, we must take conscious action toward accepting others, whether they're ethnically different than us, from a different Christian tradition or of a different generation. We need to ask ourselves if we really want to accept others, or if our call for diversity in our churches is merely a coy effort to appear politically correct. Being agents of reconciliation can manifest itself in both little and big ways. We need to start socializing with people from other ethnic groups and ecclesial traditions. Try calling a local church that isn't a part of your denomination or tradition and asking if there are Bible studies you can participate in. Invite a neighbor of a different ethnicity over for dinner and then invite them over again a few weeks later (because reconciliation isn't achieved through a one-time dinner party). Start bugging your pastoral staff about creating ecumenical events for the community. Eventually they'll get the message that you're looking for opportunities to demonstrate Christ's reconciliation in your community.

Until we are genuinely willing to embrace diversity on a personal, ecclesial and societal level, we're only preaching the gospel with words. True acceptance means unconditionally loving those who are not like us. Again, if this is to become a reality in our own lives and churches, we must first embrace Christ's reconciliation, and then in turn offer this loving acceptance to those around us. When we as Christians begin to take our vocation of reconciliation seriously, the possibilities of how the Holy Spirit will move are limitless. I'm willing to bet that in 1940 when Brother Roger moved to Taizé, no one could have predicted that his desire for reconciliation and loving acceptance of others would spawn into one of the most influential ecumenical movements in the history of the church. Who knows what God might accomplish through the present-day church if we begin to take Christ's call to reconciliation seriously?

FREEDOM AND PEACE

When a pilgrim enters the community of Taizé for the first time, *freedom* might not seem like a word that they would associate with their experience, especially since the rules and boundaries of the community are explained soon after a pilgrim is greeted and placed in a welcome group. Between a walk-through of the daily schedule and the expectations the brothers have for their visitors, it wouldn't be surprising if many pilgrims initially felt constrained in Taizé. Ironically, however, the exact opposite is true. Overall, pilgrims in Taizé don't feel restricted, limited or controlled. Despite the expectation to work in the community and participate in the prayers three times a day and the Bible Introduction sessions, the young people I interviewed actually commented that they experienced a sense of freedom they'd never felt before.

I wondered if my interviews would evoke grumbling and complaining about the work or the expectation of going to prayers, but they didn't. In fact, many of the young people thrived on the structure set in place by the brothers. They actually liked going to everything. I think a large part of their desire to participate in the community is that they feel free in Taizé, because even though the brothers encourage their visitors to participate in everything, there is no one monitoring them, watching what they're doing or checking up on them. Outside of the prayers three times a day, the dorm rooms are open and the young people can return as they choose. Amazingly, very few young people actually skip the prayers and the Bible Introductions. When I went to Taizé with my family, it was during a week where there weren't any special offerings for children. Consequently, I stayed with Judah while Shannon went to her Bible Introduction. I was taken aback by how few young people there are roaming the grounds during the sessions. Somehow, the boundaries that the brothers have established offer guidance and freedom for the pilgrims. The freedom to follow the life of the community is part of what makes Taizé what it is.

While this freedom in Taizé exists purposefully, it should not be understood as liberty for individuals to do whatever they want. The brothers give the young people freedom, but not without boundaries. For example, although the brothers sell alcoholic beverages at the Oyak, pilgrims can only consume a small amount of beer or wine in the fenced-in boundaries of this area, and only during limited times of the day. Young people are free to consume alcohol, but there are boundaries set in place that prevents pilgrims from abusing it.

In many ways, this sort of ethos mirrors the freedom the brothers experience in their community. For them, following the Rule of the community is part of that freedom. In *The Rule* Brother Roger wrote:

You fear that a common rule may stifle your personality, whereas its purpose is to free you from useless shackles, so that you may better bear the responsibility of the ministry and make better use of its boldness. Like every Christian, you must accept the tension between the total freedom given by the Holy Spirit and the impossibilities in which you find yourself due to your neighbour's and your own fallen nature.[5]

Like all monastic movements, the brothers do not view their Rule as something that strips them of their freedom, but as a vehicle that grants them the freedom to love and serve in a way that honors Christ's love and cultivates a spirit of responsibility. The essence of the Rule seeks only to delineate "the minimum [that is] necessary for a community seeking to build itself in Christ, and to give itself up to a common service of God."[6]

Young people also experience freedom in Taizé as being free *from.* Being free to do or not do something is only one facet of freedom. Freedom *from* something is a biblical concept that spans the breadth of the canon. Scripture tells us the story of our freedom from bondage. We are freed from sin because of Christ's death on the cross. He freed us from our slavery to sin and death. In Taizé, young people are reminded of that freedom. They are no longer bound by the ecclesial and societal structures that seem to oppress them. The young

Les jeunes in a sharing group

people in Taizé are free to pray and fellowship with other believers.

Without question, this sense of freedom stems from the spirit of reconciliation that characterizes the Taizé community. Reconciliation and freedom cannot be understood apart from one another. For example, Thomas, a twenty-six-year-old from Bavaria, visited Taizé seventeen times throughout his life because his parents brought him there when he was a young child. Consequently, the Taizé community has become a significant part of his spiritual formation. In describing why he returns to Taizé on his own, he used phrases like, "Here, I am free" and "Taizé is a kind of utopia for me." Another young man named Jöchem, from Belgium, echoed Thomas's sentiments: "In Taizé we are free not to hate. . . . It doesn't exist here. . . . It's a paradise on earth." Though Jöchem could not articulate the palpable relationship between freedom and acceptance at Taizé, in his eyes, people treated each other differently in the community. Jöchem said that while he has "always been a 'Christian,' [at Taizé he is] now beginning to believe and realize what faith in Christ really is." Put differently, for Thomas, Jöchem and many others the experience of acceptance and reconciliation begot a sense of freedom, which in turn created a sense of Christian euphoria. Taizé was one of the only places on earth that they felt this free.

I too encountered this feeling of freedom, but in a very different manner than many pilgrims. Because I was researching the community, my eyes and ears were in tune to what makes Taizé tick. The notion of freedom continually surfaced, not just in my interviews with young pilgrims but also in the words of the brothers in the Bible Introductions and in our conversations. For example, the day after Brother Roger's death, during the adult Bible Introduction, a German brother addressed the feelings and struggles that many of us were facing. He graciously answered all the questions we had about Brother Roger's murder, and though he was somber he was noticeably void of hatred, malice, resentment and vengeance. Furthermore, he had a distinctive aura of love and freedom about him. He didn't display the normal heaviness that one might associate with the loss of a loved one. From the quality of his voice to his body language, he emitted a sense of peace—extending it to all those who were present that day.

Unbeknownst to me at that time, this brother's response to this tragedy embodied a theme that I repeatedly observed in my research. The brothers assured

Brother Roger's burial cross

us that we were welcome to remain in the community, because they considered the loss of Brother Roger's life our loss as well.

The German brother repeatedly emphasized the freedom we have been given in Christ. He said that we were "free to forgive," "free to love" and "free to embrace others because Christ freely embraced us." His emphasis on freedom stood out to me that day, not only because their beloved founder and prior was taken from them the night before, but also because it seemed so contrary to what we would expect. Perhaps it wasn't only his words that struck me as surprising, but also the apparent spirit of peace that seemed to reside in him. To be honest, it was rather disorienting. I overheard many discussions that week about the strange sense of peace that seemed to dwell with the brothers. I know I didn't feel free or a sense of peace, yet they did. They were free to accept us in the midst of their loss and they were free to embrace the Romanian pilgrims visiting that week with open arms. This freedom, however, extends beyond the daily structure and ethos of the community and actually penetrates the most sacred part of the community: the prayers. Many pilgrims linked their experience of freedom with the prayers.

When you walk into the Church of Reconciliation, *freedom* and *peace* are two words that capture the setting with uncanny precision. From the moment your eyes view the choir, a sense of freedom fills your being. The area is open for pilgrims to find a space from which to pray. As the prayers begin, people are free to sing or to listen. There is no predetermined application for the Scripture reading that is imposed upon the visitors. During the silence, there is no prescribed activity that is expected to take place. This sort of freedom is unknown in many of our traditional and contemporary services in Western Christianity. At Taizé, however, young and old alike are free to experience the holy, encounter the sacred and touch the living God.

The natural outcome of this freedom is peace. In my interviews young people repeatedly associated their experience in Taizé with peace. Thomas and Jöchem are a good example of how powerful this can be for pilgrims. In the midst of the craziness of their lives in their home countries, these two young men returned to Taizé again and again in large part because it was where they felt at peace with God, with others and with themselves.

What can we learn from this sense of freedom that is so readily available at Taizé? I believe there are several things. First, one of the primary reasons young people feel free at Taizé is because of the "permeable boundaries" that exist. Young people are given freedom in worship. They are given the opportunity to move toward God at their own pace.

In many churches, rather than offering young people permeable boundaries that afford them real freedom we err by either removing all boundaries or making the constraints of worship too rigid. Often parents remove all expectations for their youth to participate in the life of church. Teenagers are allowed to choose to come to church or to remain at home. If the life of the church doesn't connect with them, young people exercise their freedom by opting out. On the other hand, many parents force their teenagers to participate in the life of the church. They make church attendance compulsory and often enforce it with an iron hand. Unfortunately, beyond parents' spiritual enforcements, a specific denomination's worship style often sets the limits of a young person's spiritual searching or expression.

Rather than offering young people too much freedom or forcing them to engage in worship, perhaps we should offer them freedom within the boundaries of our ecclesial communities. If young people were able to experience freedom within the walls of the church and were able to approach God with permeable boundaries, more of them would encounter the Holy Spirit in a direct and personal way. In order for this to happen, however, I believe we need to glean another lesson from Taizé, namely, the importance of sacred space.

In Taizé, young people are given space to pursue God. They are given the freedom to sit, wait and listen. In many of our churches today, however, we force-feed our young people the ways of our particular tradition. Rather than offering them sacred space to explore their spirituality, we ask them to fit into a preshaped mold. For example, confirmation in many churches aims at making youth mature and knowledgeable Christians in our particular vein of the faith. In some sense, our trajectory is more indoctrination with the aim of membership than formation with the goal of identity transformation. Do we want young people who understand their call and vocation as one of reconciliation or do we want members on a membership roll to perpetuate the embodied life of our congregations? Don't get me wrong, membership in a Christian community is a perfectly acceptable aim, but not at the expense of an authentic Christ-centered belonging. Perhaps it's time to give our young people some space—or better yet, perhaps it's time to give the Holy Spirit a chance to enliven our young people to a living relationship with a transcendent God.

Finally, if we're going to be truly honest with ourselves we have to ask if our churches really extend God's peace to all our members. Let's face it, we live in a crazy society that is filled with endless interruptions and distractions. The communal life in Taizé not only offers young people freedom *to* search, they also offer all pilgrims freedom *from* what seeks to constrain and oppress them. We need to take a hard look at our churches and ask ourselves if we offer young people freedom from the pressures of the world. Are there sacred times and spaces in our churches where young people can escape the media-saturated, consumer-driven, marketing society? Or do we offer them a second-rate version of what the world offers them? What if our young people were offered a sacred space where they could be silent? Instead of importing only the chants of Taizé for our worship, perhaps we should also consider adopting their sense of time and space for young people to explore the faith and the beauty of our traditions. Over 100,000 young people come to Taizé each year. Could it be that they're not coming for the chants but instead for the sense of freedom and peace they find in a community personified by reconciliation and acceptance? Before I carry this line of thought any farther, I must address one final theme—trust.

Trust and Responsibility

Many young people who come on spiritual pilgrimages from around the globe are often seeking something greater than what their churches are offering them. What they find at Taizé is an ecumenical community that openly welcomes them into their communal life, and genuinely trusts them enough to share in the communal work of a life together. As I said before, the brothers expect young people to participate in the work of the community—some of them might even be asked to begin their work a few hours after they arrive by helping out with the evening meal. At the core of this expectation, however, is a profound *trust* in young people.

When travelers ascend the hill for the first time, the trust and level of responsibility offered takes them by surprise. One Swedish youth confessed:

> I think somehow since I did not have that expectation, when I came to Taizé and I saw that it's not like I imagined . . . I felt very open for everything, and when then they say that "Well . . . during this week you will participate in prayers and Bible Introduction and also *work.*" . . . Of course I'm not used to doing that much work at home . . . so maybe it was a bit weird, like 'why should I clean?' but of course since I get the food and since this now feels like my home—but of course it's not my home . . . so of course I need to help and make sure that everything works and you have to do your job.

While it is surprising for some that upon their arrival at Taizé, guests are expected to sign up for a work team, young people often recognize the responsibility being given to them through their job in the community. Western culture often lacks an authentic trust of young people, so it's not shocking that young people are astonished by the brothers' willingness to trust them, even before they really know them. At Taizé trust is given, *not* earned.

As I stated earlier, each week at Taizé the pilgrims accomplish all of the work that is required to operate this ecumenical community. Teams of young people clean the grounds daily. Some sweep and pick up trash, while others clean the bathrooms. Still others are stationed at the welcome center or on the night welcome team to patrol the community until the morning. Young people work in the Oyak or the Exposition as well, while a large number help with the functioning of the prayer times (from handing out songbooks to making sure people are quiet). Many others participate in a myriad of other smaller tasks around the grounds. During any week of the summer, there could be up to six thousand visitors at Taizé, and these guests are fed from start to finish by young people—three meals a day! A team of youth prepares the food for cooking, and another team cooks it; a different team serves the meal, while yet another washes up both the cooking dishes and the guests' dishes as well. Young people contribute to almost every aspect of the community. During the coldest winter months, when the guest count is often under a hundred people, the visitors are still responsible for every aspect of their life together.

In talking with one of the brothers, I asked him why he thought young people continue to come in hoards to a simple community that expects so much from them. He replied, "They are given responsibility." While responsibility does provide teenagers with a sense of connection to something greater than themselves, to name the work as one of Taizé's more alluring characteristics for young people seemed counterintuitive. But to the brothers, a young person is central to the community when he or she serves others in both meaningful and banal ways; it is in pilgrims' work that they are serving both Christ and one another at the same time.

Overall, the young people that I interviewed were very positive about the shared communal work at Taizé. Not only did they see it as necessary for practical reasons, but they also genuinely enjoyed participating in the communal life in this way. I got a general sense that many of them truly believed the brothers trusted them. This genuine expression of trust gave these young people a feeling of significance in the community, a significance that wasn't derived from feeling like they were special and that the whole community would collapse if they failed to do their job, but rather from understanding that they were a small part of a larger mechanism that relied heavily upon everyone fulfilling their role.

The more I've pondered this phenomenon the more convinced I am that there is a distinct relationship between trust and responsibility at Taizé. Brother Roger often wrote and spoke about trust, and at Taizé, one of the most tangible ways trust is realized is in the practice of shared communal work. Orsi, a Hungarian woman who with her husband coordinates most of the work related to food for the community, recalled Brother Roger saying, "I'm ready to go to the end of the world to shout my trust in young people." Brother Roger was able to identify something in young people that many others overlook.

Another result of the trust the brothers demonstrate for young people is a greater sense of belonging. While the prayers connect them to God, the work connects them to each other. Several young people commented that they felt a deeper sense of community in their work groups than they did in any other aspect of Taizé's communal life. For many young people this sort of shared work redefined their understanding of community. One brother commented:

> People tell us that *work* is one thing they appreciate, that they don't feel like consumers, its not just something that's put on for them . . . somehow they're called . . . as much as they can . . . they're called to take on some responsibility . . . I think people appreciate that, it makes them feel like they count.

For many of the young people that I interviewed, it was through the work that they experienced a greater sense of belonging. They were genuinely needed. In caring for one another, young people experience community.

While this may seem like a simple concept, as I pondered the relationship that churches have with their young people, I'm not sure that we really allow young people to care for one another and for us. Two key factors from Taizé can help us in this area. First, in Taizé young people are called to a purpose in community and trusted enough to live in the reality of that calling. Do we as theologians, practitioners and lay Christians really trust young people in our churches? The brothers trust the young people who come from the very beginning. They are given tasks without any reference to past failures or shortcomings. I have an inclination that this trust contributes significantly to the identity of the young people who visit Taizé each year. If they don't feel trusted in their home religious environments but do feel trusted in Taizé, it's only logical to conclude that this community would resonate with a deeper longing in their spirits.

After the murder of Brother Roger in August of 2005, the brothers' trust in their visitors was even more remarkable and noticeable. No barricades were erected and no security measures were taken to insure the safety of the community from that point forward. They are open to harm. The brothers believe this is part of their calling in life—to trust those whom they have no reason to trust. Essentially, this is the manner in which God relates to us. God trusts humans to communicate the gospel to a lost and dying world, despite our depravity and the sinfulness we live in each day. The risk of failure is great, but the trust that is exhibited is more powerful in the end. I believe young people feel this in the Taizé community—and I believe young people long for this connection to one another in our churches as well.

Second, in Taizé young people experience a deep sense of belonging, a sense of intimacy with others and with God, that partly stems from their participation in shared communal work. They are called to serve each other in a way that is uncommon to them. In our ecclesial settings we rarely ask young people to serve one another. We might occasionally ask them to serve the larger congregation through various roles in the liturgy or in a special project in the church, but are they really learning to serve each other?

Missions trips are one of the main ways we try to help young people serve. We ask them to give up a week during their summer to serve those who are less fortunate, and we use the trips to remind them of the blessings we've been given and to mobilize them to be more magnanimous. It could be argued that we are attempting to build their character. The problem with this sort of isolated service to others is it does not teach young people the joy of serving their *neighbors*. If they're only engaged in this type of service toward the poor and needy we risk linking their servanthood solely to their charity. We trust young people to serve those less fortunate—but do we trust them enough to serve the church in all its capacities and functions? A tough question, no doubt, but one that must be considered.

In Taizé, young people serve others because that's what is required to sustain life. There is no one else to do the work, thus a shared communal work ethic is mandatory for the daily functioning of the community. While there is a practical side to that need, which many young people realize once they're in the community, there is a greater reality that is enacted in serving one another. Not only is a greater sense of belonging and community created in the smaller work teams, but knowing that you are part of a larger whole fosters a greater understanding of your role, responsibility and relationship to others.

WHAT ARE WE IMPORTING?

I believe the three themes of *reconciliation, freedom* and *trust* stand out as the most important aspects of the community for young people. While they may not say it in such a concise manner, their stories and testimonies about participating in the community reveal that these characteristics have helped form them spiritually. Taizé is a community of reconciliation first and foremost, and from this reconciliation, loving acceptance is born. Even more, when loving acceptance is authentically extended, a sense of freedom and peace is procured. When these themes are coupled with the genuine trust that the brothers offer young people, it should come as no surprise that young pilgrims make their way back to the hill, year after year.

Saddened as I am to say it, by and large, many churches have missed the boat when it comes to these themes. Even those pastors, priests, worship leaders and youth ministers who come to Taizé each year make their way in and out of the community without realizing the significance of such themes. Instead, we attempt to import one of the most tangible aspects of the community—the prayers—without adopting other powerful aspects of Taizé. In all fairness, the brothers do make it easy for Christians to import and to some extent implement a prayer service using the chants. In the Exposition, you can purchase the music, CDs, songbooks, candles, icons and even a giant poster of the Taizé cross. Even with these tools, however, church leaders will never be able to capture the essence of the Taizé prayers unless they begin to consider what lies behind the chants.

For the first nine chapters of this book, I have pored over the endless details of the community's life and liturgy. In the final chapter I offer my thoughts on how you can use the chants with respectful regard to Taizé. But I hope you've been able to catch a glimpse of a humble group of men who've changed the history of the world in a very profound way—not from their chants, but through their obedience to Christ's call to be reconcilers for God.

10

Importing Taizé

Let your servant now go in peace, O Lord,
now go in peace according to your word.

۞

Without a doubt, the Taizé chants have made their way into the North American understanding of spirituality. It's not hard to find a church or college that's offering a worship service inspired by the community. Truth be told, before I sat down to write this chapter I decided to Google the word *Taizé* plus the names of various cities where people I know live. Within a matter of minutes, I located Taizé worship services or Taizé-style services near Columbus and Cincinnati, Ohio; Indianapolis, Indiana; Wheaton, Illinois; Minneapolis, Minnesota; Seattle, Washington; in my hometown, Princeton, New Jersey; and many more. These services ranged from simple to elaborate. Most used live musicians. Some mentioned candles. A few actually referred to the Taizé community. One said that it was a nondenominational service. The majority of these services were held once a month. If I were to do a census of how many Taizé-style services occur in North American cities, I'm willing to bet that we'd be surprised at the rate at which this "style" of worship has spread.

What my census couldn't accurately track, however, would be how many of these worship services have actually endured the test of time. Unfortunately, I know of too many prayer services using the Taizé chants that were begun with big hopes of attracting the masses, but drew only a few. These endeavors didn't fail because they "weren't doing the chants right" or because they picked a bad night. In most cases, waning attendance was the culprit. We live in a disposable utilitarian society. If a new program or service doesn't accomplish the anticipated results quickly, it's often cut. Such is the case with many churches that begin these prayer services with great enthusiasm and then lose momentum a month or two into the endeavor.

There are success stories however. Several churches around the country have had tremendous turnouts for their "Taizé services." For example, the Church of the Ascension, a Roman Catholic church in Oak Park, Illinois, has hosted Taizé prayers for the past fifteen years. What started out as a small prayer service primarily attended by Catholic adults has blossomed into an ecumenical worship service spanning the Christian traditions and the generational divide. In fact, it is one of the most well-attended services in the country.

This is in part due to the vision and commitment of Alec Harris and Bob Batastini, the president/CEO and the retired vice president and senior editor of GIA Publications, Inc. GIA (originally the Gregorian Institute of America) is a sacred music and music education company located in Chicago, which has sought to offer liturgical music to churches around the globe since 1941. While both men played a significant role in bringing the Taizé chants to North America, Bob Batastini was the pivotal figure in importing the music to the United States.

In 1979 Bob was visiting Joseph Gelineau, a French Jesuit priest and composer, at the Eglise Saint-Ignace in Paris (St. Ignatius Church, which is the headquarters for French Jesuits). During his visit he was introduced to none other than the famous French composer Jacques Berthier, who by this time had already composed a solid repertoire of chants for the brothers. The year prior to this meeting, the brothers had made their first recording of the chants in the Notre Dame Cathedral. The meeting didn't strike Bob as significant until he returned home to Chicago and read an article about the Taizé community that also mentioned Jacques Berthier. Bob quickly sent the article to Berthier and soon after received a small parcel containing two LPs and four little books written by Brother Roger. When Bob listened to the LPs, he knew right away that he needed to import the music to North America.

Within a few short weeks, Bob had contacted the community and discussed the possibility of becoming Taizé's North American distributor. Moreover, he inquired about reprinting some of their written material. Through a back-and-forth exchange of phone calls and visits, Bob formed a friendship with the brothers. Ever since 1979, GIA Publications has been the primary distributor of Taizé's books and music in North America. While I wouldn't want to give sole credit to Bob Batastini and GIA Publications for spreading the Taizé chants throughout the United States and Canada, they certainly played a key role in our growing fascination with the community. We should, however, also examine a larger contextual shift in the North American ecclesial landscape over the past two decades.

Moving Toward the Contemplative

During the 1990s, a steady shift occurred in the way North American Christians conceptualize their faith. As the baby boomers took the helm of our churches, they successfully navigated the "hows" of marketing Christ to the culture, and as a consequence we saw an emergence of the consumer-driven megachurch paradigm. Many of our larger churches became mini-malls, hosting coffee shops, bookstores and hair salons. Business-style structures seeped into the polity and life of the church, and self-help Christianity became not only acceptable but the norm. Between mission statements, "purpose"-oriented spiritual formation and rediscovered biblical prayers guaranteeing prosperity, we found ourselves in a whirlwind of "progress" in our understanding of what it means to be the body of Christ in a secular culture. What seemed like a marketing version of the Great Awakening, however, left much to be desired for many young people.

While baby boomers have been hopping and swapping church member-ship, sociologists and church leaders alike have observed that Generation X and Millennials are unsettled with the current marketing-oriented approach to the spiritual life. There are many factors that have played a role in this perception of North American religion, but this book unfortunately is not the place for that discussion. Several insightful books, however, do speak to this issue in a very lucid, albeit poignant way.[1]

This spiritual discontentment in young people may not be apparent to many evangelical churches that have seen Gen X ministries thrive over the past decade, but for many mainline Protestant and Catholic churches, this discontentment has felt like a heavy hand of oppression. There are countless testimonies to the hemorrhaging of young people from our churches. How have they dealt with this mass exodus? For mainline Protestant churches, in particular, adaptation to the seeker-sensitive, marketing model has characterized their efforts. While most mainline churches haven't taken it to the extremes that growing evan-gelical churches have, we've unquestionably seen a rise in "program-oriented" ecclesiology. The capitalistic ideal of "if you build it they will come" has personified our efforts to reconnect our younger generations with the church and with God. Pastors, church leaders and elders are consumed with making sure our churches have enough programs to draw young families and youth into the pastoral fold.

By the turn of the millennium, we started to see the effects of this dis-satisfaction. While some young people began turning toward alternative religions, many young adults have abandoned institutional religion alto-gether. They haven't done away with spirituality per se; in fact, spirituality is undoubtedly present in the lives of Gen Xers and Millennials. It's present, however, in a slightly different format than many pastors and church leaders expected. Within the diversity of our younger generations, we have seen growing interest in contemplative spirituality. While this often finds its ex-pression in New Age spirituality and Buddhism, there is a sizable cohort of young adults turning to more ancient liturgies and prayer practices.

A renewed interest in High-Church ecclesiology has even been observed.[2] Sacramental theology and the early church have proven to be hot topics among young people. Likewise, ancient and medieval practices have infiltrated the spiritual lives of these generations. Take practices like the Ignatian examen, the Jesus Prayer and *lectio divina* for example. I can't tell you how many times and in how many variations I've seen the ancient practice of *lectio divina* utilized in Christian settings.

Interest in monasticism and intentional communities is also on the rise. This trend is verifiable not only by the proliferation of books about the monastic movement, new monasticism and contemplative ministry, but also by the emergence of smaller intentional communities around the country. At the core of this interest, we find young adults longing for something greater than the current offerings on the buffet of the ecclesial marketplace. I believe this is a large part of the reason we've seen a significant rise in interest about Taizé in North America.

For many mainline Protestant and Catholic churches, Taizé is an acceptable bridge between our emphasis on our tradition and the history of the Christian church. Church leaders, Protestant and Catholic alike, know about the hoards of young people drawn to Taizé each year. As they try to find ways to reach the young adults of our generation, they wonder whether they'll get the same results as Taizé has if they provide their local context a comparable offering.

The problem, however, is that the music of Taizé has become highly disconnected from the origin of its inception: the community. In some of our churches, the Taizé chants have become a gimmick for reaching young people. The rationale behind this use of the chants is somewhat justifiable if all we know about the music is that it's associated with an ecumenical monastic movement in France that attracts a lot of young people. After all, if these repetitive chants work for some ecumenical "monks," why wouldn't we get the same result? There are countless churches who believe the moment they dim the lights, light a few dozen candles, display a few icons and play the Taizé chants, droves of young adults will fill their churches to the brim. Unfortunately, this isn't how it works. Others pop a Taizé chant into the normal liturgy of their Sunday services hoping that this effort will be enough to offer a breath of the contemplative without upsetting the expectations of older generations. As a consequence of these efforts, we deprive ourselves of the very heart of the chants.

What I'm saying is this: there is no formula that will make the Taizé chants work in our congregations, primarily because there is no formula that makes the Taizé community work. What we can surmise, as I purported in the previous chapter, is that there are themes that run deep in the community and which ultimately offer young people something greater than themselves—Christ's work of reconciliation. With that said, I'm sure that some of you are wondering, *But how can we use the chants then?* I'm so glad you asked.

Using the Taizé Chants Faithfully

After speaking about the community, I'm often asked the same question of how can we use the chants faithfully. While I do believe there are more faithful ways to use the community's chants in local churches than the way many are currently using them, I don't want to promote myself as an authority on "correctly" employing the Taizé chants in your congregations. Remember, the chants evolved out of the needs of a particular context; thus, if they are used in a particular context, they need to find an expression that reflects the uniqueness of that environment. Chances are, even if you follow some of the suggestions I'm going to offer, you might not accomplish what you're hoping to see happen. For this reason, I believe it's worthwhile to begin this section by asking the question "Why do you want to use the Taizé chants?"

As stated above, many church leaders simply would like to see young people return to their churches. A noble desire indeed, however, it shouldn't warrant a "by any means necessary" tactic. We won't grow our churches by implementing the Taizé chants or any other type of ancient practice. In the end, those types of efforts really never accomplish what's at the core of our desires.

Other leaders might simply want to foster a greater sense of contemplative spirituality in their congregations. This too is a worthy impetus, however, we must remember that the contemplative life of a church cannot be air-dropped in like a food shipment in war-torn areas of the world. This tactic may tease an interest in contemplative practices, but when it has run its course, something new will take its place. A life of spiritual contemplation is nurtured from a desire to escape the busyness of the world, for the gospel's sake. A life of contemplation longs for the presence of God to saturate our souls. While I still believe this is at the core of all Christians' hearts, for many congregations this desire must be drawn out through the gradual integration of spiritual practices—not as gimmicks, but as sacramental rhythms in our communal life together.

What it really boils down to is that we need to ask ourselves what we want for ourselves, our families, our churches and the spiritual lives of our communities. At the heart of the Taizé community, there exists an unquenchable longing for reconciliation on earth. This is not a humanly constructed aim but is found in the heart of the gospel. In 2 Corinthians 5:17-20 it says:

> So if anyone is in Christ, there is a new creation: everything old has passed away; see, everything has become new! All this is from God, who *reconciled* us to himself through Christ, and has given us the ministry of *reconciliation;* that is, in Christ God was *reconciling* the world to himself, not counting their trespasses against them, and entrusting the message of *reconciliation* to us. So we are ambassadors for Christ, since God is making his appeal through us; we entreat you on behalf of Christ, be *reconciled* to God. (NRSV, italics mine)

If we're going to import anything from the Taizé community, perhaps we ought to import their emphasis on reconciliation. Do we really long for the world to be reconciled to God? Or better yet, do we really want our own hearts to be reconciled to our Creator? As I stated in the last chapter, there is a cost in becoming a sign of reconciliation to the world. Before we try out any other outreach tactics, we need to look inward and ask what we hope to accomplish by importing the Taizé chants. I genuinely believe that if we first ask ourselves this question, the Taizé chants will have a new meaning. We will begin to see their function in the life of our churches in a new light. When our churches become communities of reconciliation, the chants can be seen as an expression of that calling.

In other words, if we are going to faithfully use the chants, we must begin by asking how we can usher reconciliation into our churches and our communities. This has tremendous implications for how we "do" ministry. It might mean that our various traditions need to begin praying together; it might mean that we need to plant our next church in poor areas of our cities; and it might mean that we have to stop viewing youth and children's ministry as belonging in our church basements.

Becoming a community of reconciliation won't happen overnight. Remember that the Taizé community didn't just spring up. It started with one man's longing to be a sign of reconciliation in the world. Nine years after Brother Roger moved to Taizé, there were only a dozen brothers. By current North American standards, his growth rate wasn't too impressive. In fact, if Brother Roger had begun his ministry in our consumer-oriented culture with our Western capitalistic ideals, we would have told him to throw the towel in by now. It's a good thing that Brother Roger wasn't concerned with being successful.

Trust me, it's a hard leap to make. As a youth minister, the success of my ministry was always judged by how many youth I had each week. I often wonder what my earlier ministry would have been like had I just determined to be faithful to what Christ has called me to do. You can read what follows—how to "do" the chants with regard to the community—with or without embracing the Christian vocation of reconciliation, but I can promise you this: If you take seriously Christ's call for us to become ambassadors of reconciliation, it won't matter how well you use the chants, because in time, they will become an expression of your deepest longing to see all reconciled in Christ Jesus.

The Chants in Context

Once you've determined why you're using the chants, you need to decide what context you'll use them in. As a pastor, are you simply trying to integrate a contemplative piece into your Sunday morning worship? Are you looking to form a monthly contemplative service to offer your congregation a wider variety of expressions of worship? Perhaps you're in the Catholic tradition and you're using the chants as an extension of the church's prayer life, or maybe you're a student at a college or seminary and you desire to bring other contemplative seekers together. Whatever the reason, you'll have to determine the context in which the chants will be utilized: Sunday service, contemplative service, extra prayer service, college outreach, or otherwise. Try and keep your context in mind as you plan the prayer times.

Naturally, if you have a group of people who are familiar with Taizé and desire to begin praying together using the chants, your work is half done. If, however, your desire is to introduce Taizé chants to others in your church, small group or community, I would urge you to begin by having an informative meeting where you share about the community, its history, the way the prayers have developed and what makes the Taizé community so unique. With these things in mind, you'll be able to start your prayer gathering with some context undergirding the chants. If your goal is to start a prayer time for the larger community, I would also suggest that you first contact some of the other denominations and Christian traditions in your town to find out if they'd like to begin praying together. In fact, when Protestants ask me what the first thing that they need to do is to start a "Taizé service" (something which both excites me and makes me cringe a little), I usually respond, "Find a Catholic church and ask them if they'd be interested in praying together using the Taizé chants." When my Catholic friends ask me the same question, I in turn point them toward Protestant churches. While I can't guarantee the responses you will receive, I'm willing to bet that your inquiry will begin to break down barriers. Knowing whom you'll be praying with will help you focus on how you want to invite people to the prayers.

Once you've determined whom you'll gather with, the next step is deciding how often your group will meet. While there are a few "Taizé services" that occur weekly, monthly ones are more common. If all you're attempting to do is introduce the Taizé prayers to your church as a means of contemplative worship, meeting monthly might be sufficient. Be aware, though, that monthly gatherings rarely foster a sense of community because of the lack of continuity.

If your desire is to be a sign of reconciliation in your community, meeting weekly is a more appropriate choice. Weekly meetings offer those who gather a chance to develop relationships with one another. Moreover, in North America gathering at least once a week is understood as a legitimate commitment to something. Take church, for example. Those who gather at least once a week are looked at as committed members of the church. If our members only showed up once a month, however, their commitment level might be in question.

If you live in a college or seminary community, it might even be possible to gather daily or during the weekdays. Personally, I think that this is the best option, although I am aware of the difficulties that it presents for peoples' schedules. Part of the reason the prayers are so influential in Taizé is because the brothers' lives are centered around them. Three times a day the community gathers to pray. The frequency offers the community a rhythm of life that is infused with prayer. While in Taizé, it's almost impossible to get the chants out of your mind; there is always one lingering in the back of your head. This repetition and frequency of prayer offers Christians a tangible understanding of Paul's call for us to "pray without ceasing." In the end, you'll have to decide how much is doable for those with whom you'll be gathering.

CREATING A SACRED SPACE

Another aspect you might want to consider when you're planning to begin using the Taizé chants is where you will hold the prayers. We all know the old adage: location, location, location. As you select a room or building, consider how the space will usher those who gather into the holy. Can the room be transformed into a sacred space? While you can hold the prayers anywhere, some spaces are more conducive to prayer than others. In Taizé, most of the aesthetics operate on two principles: simplicity and beauty. While you don't have to use the same criteria for your prayer space, I would suggest choosing an area that is not cluttered with lots of visual distractions. Thus, a children's education room in your church is probably not the best place for the prayers, as caricatures of biblical figures and the second-grade class's artwork of Daniel and the lion's den hung across the wall are probably not the most helpful in creating a sacred space. If you are planning on gathering with another Christian tradition, you might want to consider rotating the prayer time between the two churches. While it does make knowing the schedule a tad hectic, it speaks volumes about your hope for ecumenism.

As you consider the aesthetics of the room, pay attention to whether there is ample floor space. In leading Taizé prayers many times myself, I've noticed that people often have apprehensions about sitting on the floor. While it's not mandatory, I would highly recommend it. Pews and chairs have a way of making a space seem constrained. Even if you scatter chairs across the room, there are still boundaries that prohibit the natural freedom that sitting on the floor offers. That said, however, it is important that you do offer some chairs or benches for those who might find it physically difficult to sit for longer periods of time on the floor. If the room you're using has cold tile floors, you might want to think about purchasing small rugs. Carpet stores often have sample rugs about the size of a doormat. These rugs make perfect prayer rugs while offering those who pray a little more comfort. Alternatively you could also purchase seat cushions or prayer stools. When I led weekly prayers at Princeton University a few years ago, I asked a neighbor if he could build me some prayer stools. With some tools, a plank of wood, and a few screws a prayer stool can be constructed for less than ten dollars. Whatever you decide to do with the seating, the most important aspect is to make sure that the space offers those who pray a feeling of freedom and peace.

There are additional ways you can help create a sacred space for your prayers. Look at the lighting in your room. Can it be dimmed or does the room only have harsh florescent lights? If your situation is more the latter case, consider using only candles. Tea lights are inexpensive when purchased in bulk, and you can pick up reasonably priced tea-light holders at most retail stores. If you are going to use candles, you might also want to consider investing in a few refillable stick lighters. Believe me, lighting a couple hundred candles in a short amount of time is no easy trick.

As you imagine this sacred space, you'll also want to consider what sort of visual stimuli you're offering. If you have access to icons, you can set them up in various locations where they'll be accessible and seen by all. You might also want to consider placing a cross in the front of the room. I don't recommend trying to re-create the look of the Church of Reconciliation, as your aim should not be to replicate a Taizé experience but to integrate a similar spirit into your gathering.

That said, there is one visual aspect in the Church of Reconciliation that is worth considering. Think about leaving the center of your space open. If you're utilizing a chancel or a stage area, remove all items from the center of the area. While not consciously on the minds of most pilgrims, I believe part of the reason the choir in the Church of Reconciliation seems so open and free is there isn't one single icon or cross drawing our attention to the center. In Taizé, that space is purposefully open to leave room for God.

MUSIC TO MY EARS

The question of how to play the music always comes up when thinking about how to use the Taizé chants in prayer. There are actually many ways you can play the music, but there's one element that is essential in preserving the spirit of the community: it's important that the musicians who lead the prayers don't become a focal point during the gathering. One of the mistakes that many churches make is placing their musicians in plain view of those who are praying. I realize if you're using an organ in a sanctuary, this might be unavoidable. But when it is possible, place your musicians—

whether they're playing the piano, flute or guitar—off to the side or even behind the assembled gathering. Taizé's music is beautiful, and when talented musicians take the stage to lead those who are praying, there is a risk that the musicians will become an unintended focal point.

The brothers play their keyboard in the midst of the assembly gathered in Taizé, but it's done in such a way that it's almost unnoticeable (unless of course you're looking for it). Likewise, if you choose to have a cantor sing the psalm or the intercessions, try to place them in the assembly of people. Nothing about the way you use the chants should direct attention toward another person or a group of musicians. This is completely contrary to the spirit of their community. In Taizé, God is at the center of the prayers, and the brothers are very careful to insure that God remains the focus throughout the liturgy. Even if your musicians and singer have this mindset, placing them in more discrete locations during the prayer time is more appropriate. The sound of the prayers should be music to your ears, not something for your eyes.

In addition, if you're using live musicians, practicing the music on a separate occasion will help the flow of the actual prayer time. My suggestion would be to practice on another day entirely, as opposed to right before the prayer gathering. Many churches have made a habit of practicing the music for the worship service directly before the actual service, but this doesn't offer those who come a little early to the gathering a place to prepare themselves for prayer. At Taizé, there is a choir practice in the afternoon, but it's not because they're going to perform; rather, it provides people with a chance to learn new chants before the prayers, which ultimately allows them to engage in prayerful singing during the prayers. Most of the music in Taizé stems from one brother, who can practice playing the music on his own. At the very least, if your musicians have to practice before the service, consider having them meet in a different room than where the prayer gathering will be held. In this way, those who wish to come early won't be witness to the musicians figuring out how best to play the music.

I would also recommend that you purchase a few Taizé CDs for the musicians so that they can listen to the rate and tempo of the music as the community would play it. In asking the brothers about their experiences in imported Taizé worship services, one of the comments that surfaced was about the way the music is played. Many services try to force the contemplative nature of the chants by playing them very slowly. While some chants were written with slower tempos, a good number of the chants were written as hymns of praise. Listening to the CDs should help the musicians gain a feel for the tempo of the songs.

How many times to repeat a chant also needs to be considered. Another brother commented on this, that in most North American gatherings, the chants aren't sung with enough repetition. I've been in services where some chants were only sung twice through. What leaders often fail to realize is that the contemplative nature of the prayer is enhanced when the chant is sung over and over again. That's not to say that you should carry on with "Ubi Caritas" for fifteen minutes; there is a sense of when a chant has been repeated enough. That too is a judgment call best suited for those who are keenly aware of the spirit of the prayers.

It's worth remembering that the chants are prayers. They were not composed only as songs, but as sung prayers. While songs can be repeated a few times over, the repetition of the Taizé chants reverberates an ancient practice of meditative prayer. Much like the Jesus Prayer ("Lord Jesus Christ, have mercy on me, a sinner"), which was repeated in almost endless succession, the Taizé chants are prayers that are meant to penetrate our spirits through each successive repetition. For many Christians, the practice of repetitive prayer seems awkward and almost mind-numbing at times; however, there is a rich reason for praying this way, especially when using the community's chants.

The repetition has a practical reason as well. Because the chants were birthed out of a need to include a multinational assembly of pilgrims, the prayers need to be sung over and over again so that people can learn them. For example, if a pilgrim from North America is trying to sing a chant in French, it may take more than a few rounds for them to even be able to pronounce some of the words. Moreover, when singing the chants in other languages, it's important for the pilgrim to have some idea what is being prayed. In the Taizé songbooks, the words of every song are included in other languages. While the translations might not be exact, it gives the pilgrim some idea of what is being sung. Between learning the melody of the prayer, pronouncing the words and having a rudimentary grasp of the meaning of the chant, only singing it for a minute or two isn't sufficient. It's important, then, that when using other languages in a predominately English-speaking prayer gathering you allow enough repetition for those praying to fully experience the prayer. While not everyone will perfect the selected chants in one setting, providing a longer exposure to the chants will help in making the prayers meaningful. That said, if you're able, choose chants that are written in English or use the English translation of a chant. This will also help those praying to connect with the meaning of the prayer.

In my opinion, there's another purpose for repeating the chants. I like to think of it as a process through which the words of the prayer gain meaning for the person singing it. As I've experienced it, a person will go through three stages while learning a new chant. When they first start singing, there is sometimes too much emphasis on trying to learn the song—figuring out the melody and memorizing the words. This *learning* stage can last a few minutes or longer depending on the person and the particular chant being sung.

Next comes the *lull* stage. You know when you've entered into lull stage when you're almost mindlessly singing the prayer; your mind seems to be someplace else. This is similar to when you're driving and you go into autopilot mode. Then, before you know it, you're at your destination saying to yourself, "How did I get here?" The lull stage is not a bad phase to be in because it means you're beginning to internalize the prayers. This internalizing leads you to the final stage, the *lingering* stage.

The lingering stage is reached when you're conscious of what you're singing, but you no longer have to "think" about the words or the melody. The chant is no longer a written text put to music but a living, breathing prayer that emerges from the depths of your soul. The repetition of the chant no longer matters, because you're dwelling in the presence of God. When using the Taizé chants, allow people to make their way through these three stages. Give them a chance to learn the song, allow them to pass through the lull of the repetition, and let them move into a place where they want nothing more than to linger in the presence of God.

I'm sure by now many of you are saying, "Well then how long should we repeat the chants?" Unfortunately, I can't answer that question for you. What I can do is make a suggestion that will help you gauge the length of the repetition and the flow of the prayers overall. In fact, when I've used the prayers in various settings, I've resorted to a bit of technology to help me out. My suggestion is to utilize the instrumental soundtracks put out by the community. At the time of this writing, there are two instrumental CDs available offering thirty-seven different Taizé chants without voice accompaniment. I've loaded these CDs onto my computer and created playlists with different selections of chants on them in an order that I've predetermined. I've even created a silent track to accommodate both the Scripture reading and the longer period of silence. This way, I can load the playlist on my iPod and carry the music for the entire prayer service in my pocket. With a little help from some computer speakers, I can fill a room with the instrumental tracks with the touch of a button. Although this requires some thought beforehand, it allows me to participate in the prayers without worrying what chant comes next or how long each chant should last. Furthermore, this method takes the performance aspect out of the prayer time. There are no leaders or musicians to attract attention, only the perfectly timed and executed sound of each chant.

The disadvantage of this method, however, is that I don't have the option to extend a chant or to shorten the time of silence if I feel the need. Therefore, while using an MP3 player offers portable convenience with a suitable consistency in the music, it doesn't offer me the freedom of adjusting the prayers in the moment. Some may find the playlist method somewhat lacking in authenticity and prefer to simply sing a cappella. If that is your preference, it would be worth practicing with the CDs prior to your prayer times to help you learn the melody and tempo of the chants.

However you decide to use the prayers, so long as you're sensitive to the spirit of the community and the guidance of the Holy Spirit, I'm sure that your prayer gathering will be uplifting for your local community and glorifying to God.

THE PRAYER LITURGY

Once you know who you're praying with, where you'll gather, what your sacred space will look like and how you're going to play the music, the next step is to consider the flow of the prayers. Utilizing the brothers' liturgy directly, while completely viable, is not the only option. While their simple liturgy embraces various aspects of the different Christian traditions, you might feel led to make some alterations to include an element from your own tradition. For example, in Presbyterian liturgy, a time of confession is an essential part of the communal gathering. In the context of the prayers, then, you might want to include a read confession or a short time of silence for confession. This period should not be too long, though, so that it doesn't get confused with the silence that stands in the center of the prayers. Each situation will present its own needs and liturgical particularities. You should consider these elements as you plan your prayer gathering.

Two of the elements of the Taizé liturgy in particular that should be thought through beforehand are the Scripture reading and the time of silence. As I explained in the chapter on the prayers, in Taizé the Scripture readings are selected from a two-year lectionary. Even with this guide, however, the brothers deviate from the lectionary when necessary. You should feel free to follow the lectionary of your denomination if your gathering is primarily for those from your own tradition. If you're gathering with other Christian traditions, you might want to consider using the Revised Common Lectionary, an ecumenical resource that many churches use on a weekly basis. When selecting a passage from the lectionary, it's important that you remember who is attending the prayers. Not all passages in the lectionary may seem appropriate for an ecumenical prayer service. Moreover, don't feel like you have to read the whole passage. Instead, read a reasonable amount that you feel can be digested by those gathered. You can read from a lectern or, better yet, from your place on the floor of the assembly. In this way, your presence won't become the focal point, but rather the words of the Scripture can be heard without distraction. After the Scripture reading is complete, you can sing another chant as a response or move right into the time of silence.

When "Taizé services" in North America come to the period of silence, it's often an awkward part of the liturgy—not because the silence itself is awkward, but because of how the silence is often used. In North American "Taizé services," in particular, the brothers have noticed that the time of silence is often cut short, or instead of having one longer time of silence, worship leaders intersperse several shorter periods of silence. What these leaders fail to realize is that the silence in Taizé is equivalent to the sermon in a traditional service. The silence is the point in the liturgy when pilgrims meditate on the Scripture passage and listen to the still small voice of the Holy Spirit. It is a time of waiting before God.

For many Christians, granted, this period is rather intimidating. We're not used to being silent for any length of time, and in the face of eight or ten minutes of silence, many people become anxious. In the middle of the silence they begin wondering when it will end. Each second that passes seems like an eternity. Be aware, then, that just like in Taizé, when you first introduce a period of silence it will be awkward and even scary for some.

I like to draw an analogy between this period of silence in the liturgy and bungee jumping. I know, this may seem strange, but it's actually quite fitting. When I was traveling in South Africa in the late 1990s, a few friends and I decided to pay a visit to the Bloukrans River Bridge and bungee jump the highest jump in the world (which also happens to be off the third-highest bridge in the world). It was a massive 216 meters, which is over two American football fields in length. What makes this jump particularly relevant to the chants of Taizé is what happens when a jumper is free falling. As it was explained to me by the safety crew at Bloukrans River Bridge, most commercial bungee jumps aren't high enough to break what they referred to as the terror plateau: an invisible plane that separates the free fall into two parts. It is said that the jumper is in the terror stage when he experiences overwhelming terror from jumping off the bungee platform. Having jumped off this bridge, I can vouch for the terror aspect of the jump. Because of the shorter distance of the fall in most commercial jumps, the harness starts to tighten and the jumper feels the velocity of his fall decrease before reaching the plateau. The jumper therefore never breaks this terror plateau and consequently is unable to experience the next stage of the fall, the euphoric stage. In an extremely high bungee jump, when the terror plateau is broken the jumper experiences a physical and mental elation that is most often described as being euphoric. An unexpected sense of peace and tranquility comes over the jumper in such a way that, when juxtaposed with the terror stage, seems even more profound.

I believe this is what happens when people begin to truly embrace the period of silence. At first, it's like taking a plunge into a gorge. While it's kind of exciting and perhaps a little scary to think about remaining in silence, facing the actual period of silence is rather frightening. It's like the terror stage of a bungee jump. As the period of silence begins, many people panic. They frantically ask themselves what they're supposed to be doing. Some peek at their neighbor for hints, while others try to think about other things. Some people fill this time with words, praying to God (perhaps that the silence will end soon). They keep asking themselves, "When will it end, when will it end?" Then something happens that is rightly unexplainable. They let go. They let go of their fears. They let go of their need to fill the silence with thoughts and words. They let go of wondering when the time of silence will end. When this happens a sense of peace and tranquility comes over them, much like the bungee jumper breaking through the terror plateau. This peace fills their hearts and minds so that they no longer worry about the length of the silence or what they should be doing, because they're encountering God. When those who are praying with you reach this point, the time of silence will take on a whole new meaning. This is what the brothers mean when they say that by the end of the week the pilgrims feel like the time of silence is too short.

After the period of silence, you'll have a few decisions to make. The intercessions with a response can be sung or simply read. Alternatively, you can invite others to voice their concerns and then have everyone gathered respond, "Lord, hear our prayers." Whatever method you choose to use in the intercessions, attempt to make it clear without belaboring the liturgical element with lengthy instructions. After the intercession, you can collectively say the Lord's Prayer and partake in the Eucharist if the sacrament is fitting for the prayer service. As the prayers come to a close, I would recommend allowing people to linger and leave as they feel led. If you're using live musicians, you might want to also bring a CD or MP3 player and play one of the instrumental CDs during this time. Or, if you're using an iPod, you can simply include another playlist of tracks for those who wish to remain in prayer.

Before I close this chapter, I'd like to offer one final thought. When advertising, promoting or simply telling others about your prayer service, please do not use the phrase "Taizé Prayer Service" or "Taizé-Style Prayer Service." The brothers much prefer that those who use their chants promote their gatherings simply as prayer services or prayer gatherings "with Taizé chants" or "with Taizé prayers." In this way, the emphasis of your gatherings will be on a life of contextualized prayer that just happens to use the chants of Taizé, rather than on the name of the community as a means to draw people in.

Although I've offered a lot of recommendations in this chapter for using the Taizé chants faithfully, I don't want to convey that they are the only way to do so. There are no "right ways" to use the chants; however, the ways I have just described do take into account both the community of brothers and the development of their prayers. My hope is not that you will follow my suggestions precisely but that you will thoughtfully and respectfully consider the community when you employ their chants in your worship settings and prayer services.

Epilogue

○

On my first pilgrimage to Taizé, I never imagined that I would be present for something as tragic as Brother Roger's death. The manner in which the brothers and the larger community dealt with this tragedy has had an immeasurable influence on me. Chances are, if you make it to the community sometime in your life you won't be faced with a comparable encounter— nor do you need to for it to be a life-changing visit. When sharing about my interactions with the community, people tend to assume my interest in Taizé hinges on my dramatic introduction. Frankly, I don't believe it does. Although Brother Roger's death was my entry point, it is far from being my single most defining experience on the hill. There are dozens of factors that play into how I've been transformed through my interaction with the community and the pilgrims who call it their spiritual home.

Truth be known, I really don't understand why I'm drawn to Taizé. I can pinpoint certain changes in my life since experiencing the community: I've been challenged to demonstrate more acceptance toward others. I've more fully embraced the notion of reconciliation in my understanding of Christian witness and mission. I've been confronted with the ugliness of my own consumerist tendencies. I've even pondered what it might be like to live in an intentional community here in the United States. Although I've made my most informed guess as to why people—myself included—are drawn to

Taizé, I'm positive I haven't hit the nail on the head. Perhaps because it's a nail that is not meant to be hit.

What happens at Taizé is a bit of a mystery, and maybe it should stay that way. Knowing how we've been transformed and how the formation happened are completely different. The former only requires a self-reflective spirit, whereas the latter is really in God's hands. As a practical theologian, it's actually my job to understand how formation happens, but to be honest with you, I think some things are best left unknown. While I have given you a glimpse of the communal life, the brothers' history, the development of the chants, the collective voice of hundreds of conversations and interviews, and some thoughts on what we can learn from Taizé, I still feel at a loss for words as to why 100,000 young people flock to the community each year.

What I do know is this: when I think about the Taizé community, my heart aches for the church. I often think, *What if the church could be like that?* I don't mean exactly like Taizé but more, What if the church really decided to be the church? What if the church really became a community of reconciliation? What if Roman Catholics, Protestants and Orthodox Christians really started to love and support one another? What would the church look like? I don't think the brothers are doing anything extraordinary, rather I think they're simply *doing* what Christ called us all to do—and I know that often I am not. I wonder how many other Christians in our world feel the same way I do. What I do know is that because of my encounter with the Taizé community, I long to live more faithfully to the call and vocation that God has placed on my life. Perhaps Taizé's real value is in serving as a witness that that really can be done.

The brothers have shared with me on several occasions that even if all the pilgrims stopped coming tomorrow, they would continue living their life together. They would continue praying three times a day. They would continue living among the poor. They would continue searching for ways to bring Christ's reconciliation to the world. In other words, they would continue being *faithful*. Ultimately, I think that is where we must begin. We must ask ourselves what it looks like to live faithfully in our cultural context. It may be in intentional community, but it also might not. What's important is that we seek to be faithful in all aspects of our lives. In this way, we can all be reconcilers for Christ.

While you don't need the Taizé community to realize this about our calling as Christians, it's always encouraging to see living examples of faithfulness in our world. I hope and pray that reading about their pilgrimage of trust and reconciliation has encouraged you on your own spiritual quest to incarnate Christ's love.

Appendix A

Practical Issues and Getting to Taizé

❧

Before I went on my first trip to Taizé, I asked a fellow student at Princeton Theological Seminary what I needed for my trip. Although he gave me a few pointers that were helpful, I always wished there were a more comprehensive list of pretrip recommendations available. I hope that this appendix will fill that gap for future pilgrims. In the next few pages, I'll address questions like: How do I get to Taizé? What do I need to bring with me? What should I leave behind? How much money do I need? These questions and others have frequently been asked over the past few years when I've spoke about Taizé at various junctures. I think it's helpful to know the answer to them *before* you plan a trip, rather than *discover* them once you're there.

Planning a Trip

Should I go alone or with a group?
The answer to this question is different for different people. As far as cost goes, as an individual you're not going to save any money by finding a group to go with unless it's a fairly large group, and even then the leaders' costs

are often built into the cost of the trip. So if you know you want to go, book your ticket.

The more important question you have to ask yourself is, "What do I hope to get out of this trip?" If you go with a group of people, you will inevitably bond with them during the journey. You'll spend a long voyage together getting to Taizé, and these same people will naturally become a source of community for you once you're there. This has two side effects. On the one hand, you have a safety net for fellowship in your own language, for eating with people you know and for roommates during the week. But on the other hand, it'll be harder to break away from your group and meet new people, which can be a really enriching part of the experience. Both experiences are worthwhile, so it's best to give some thought to what you're hoping to accomplish through the pilgrimage.

The international flair at Taizé is one of the peripheral draws for many young people. Despite the often difficult communication you might have with other pilgrims, there are always plenty of English-speaking Europeans who enjoy meeting native English speakers. Being alone in Taizé binds you to a much larger group of pilgrims who make their way to the community. You become one of hundreds and even thousands of searching souls. Yes, you might eat a few meals alone at the beginning of the week, but by the end of the week you find you are a part of a small network of international friends whom you've met through your work teams and sharing groups and in adjacent dorms. It's not uncommon to leave Taizé with emails from around the world. I still keep in contact with friends I've made in Taizé from Germany, Poland, Sweden, Switzerland, Canada and Ireland.

Thus the short answer to the social question is this: it depends on what you're looking for socially from your trip. If you'd like to expand your horizons a bit more and be adventurous, go alone. Alternatively, if you'd like to build or foster stronger relationships with other people from your area, go with a group. Either way, you'll still meet lots of people from other countries, but without a doubt, the social dynamics of the experience will be different depending on who you go with (or don't go with, whatever the case may be).

There are also those individuals, like pastors, church leaders and professors, who want to plan a trip to the community and are wondering if they should make a scouting trip before they take a team of people. It's a good question, as many church leaders have been exposed to "secondhand" Taizé and are a little nervous about what they'll find in the actual community. They wonder if their young people can handle the slower-paced environment (some question if their older folks can handle this as well). My recommendation for this is that leaders take a personal trip first and then bring a team back. I do understand that this is not always possible and that in many cases the church cannot afford to send their pastors and youth workers gallivanting across Europe for a week just to get a feel for a monastic community. The benefits of going alone before taking a team, however, are quite significant.

Taking a leader's trip before taking a group allows the person to really encounter the community in Taizé. Oftentimes when we are leading a trip, we forget to stop and smell the roses. Our plates are filled with details like making sure everyone has the proper documentation, checking up on our people to make sure they're doing okay, dealing with lost wallets, sickness or something else. These interruptions, while a normal and expected part of all trips, are not conducive to spiritual renewal. If group leaders can go on a preliminary trip to Taizé, it enables them to experience the prayers, work and communal life in a transformative way. It will help them plan the trip and inform the way they lead discussions about the trip. In short, a solo trip before a group trip will enrich the lives of the leaders, so that they in turn can help nurture growth in the lives of their group. For these reasons, I definitely recommend a preliminary trip for all leaders.

Are there any special considerations for leading a group to Taizé?
When bringing a group to Taizé, there are a few aspects that should be considered. First, the age range of the group carries with it several implications. For example, although younger students are allowed to visit the community, those under seventeen must be accompanied by adult leaders, which

shouldn't be a problem if you're bringing a group. The brothers do prefer young people under the age of fifteen to be accompanied by their parents, though, so if you have a mature fourteen- or fifteen-year-old, it might be advantageous to utilize their parents as adult leaders.

Young people between the ages of seventeen and twenty-nine are the ideal age to visit the community, as there are no special restrictions associated with this age group. In fact, college groups and twentysomethings form a large part of the "youth" contingent at Taizé. The brothers feel that people in this age bracket are the most receptive to searching after God. They've got a little life under their belts, and in the process of trying to form their identities, young adults begin asking questions about faith and spirituality. Somehow, where many college programs and young adult ministries falter, an ecumenical monastic community in Taizé, France, has succeeded in capturing the attention and spiritual longings of a largely forsaken generation of young people. With this in mind, if and when you are strategizing your trip, focusing on this age bracket might make your pilgrimage more relevant.

While bringing a group of pilgrims younger than seventeen poses a few restrictions, bringing a group of pilgrims older than twenty-nine also has its limitations. In fact, the brothers prefer that large groups primarily consisting of people over the age of thirty don't come. As I type this sentence I can hear some of you saying "What!?!" in a spirit of disbelief. I too was surprised to discover before my first trip to Taizé that groups of people older than thirty are highly discouraged from coming. Before I explain, it should be noted that individuals and couples who are over thirty are able to participate in the community for the week without a problem. In fact, smaller groups of four or five might even be accepted, depending on the time of year they attempt to register their visit. In a similar vein, families should also check with the community before they plan their trip, as there are certain times of the year when it's more difficult to accommodate families in the housing that's available.

The rationale for restricting groups of older pilgrims should not be simply boiled down to ageism. The brothers truly love the depth and wisdom that the older visitors bring to the pilgrim community. Moreover, it's important to them that the prayers have a multigenerational dimension, both for the young and the old. Nonetheless, the brothers have chosen to restrict the adult population in Taizé for two specific reasons.

First, if they opened their doors to adults and families without restrictions, it would be difficult to accommodate the young people. There are literally thousands upon thousands of adults who came to Taizé as young people over the past forty years. If these older pilgrims were provided with unlimited access to the community, a flood of adults would quickly wash away what has become a very sacred space for countless young people. Second, because it was young people who originally came to Taizé in search of peace and reconciliation, the brothers feel that this space must be reserved for them. Taizé offers young people a sacred space to experience God—something of extreme scarcity in our world. The brothers want to ensure that young people who want to come get that opportunity.

These are all important factors to remember when planning a trip. If you're thinking of bringing an older group to Taizé, specifically, you might want to reconsider your decision. While the brothers occasionally make exceptions for older groups, it doesn't happen all that often. If you really want to take a group of people, consider those in the seventeen to twenty-nine age bracket. It might prove to be more beneficial to all those involved in the trip.

Are there better times of the year to go to Taizé?
I wouldn't say there are better or worse times to go to the community, but there are several factors to think through. For example, weather should always be a consideration. If you're planning a trip in the summer, you risk the chance of a rainy week. Rain never affects the schedule of the day, but it does make for wet dorm rooms (although you run the risk of this affliction no matter what time of year you go). As far as temperatures go, I was there once in the summer when it was both blazing hot and frigid. So use your discretion in regards to the weather and always check the conditions for the week you'll be there before you embark on your trip.

What will play a determining factor in your experience at Taizé is the variable pilgrim population. If you're planning a trip during the summer, you should expect to face somewhere between three thousand and six thousand people, whereas if you're going in the dead of winter, you might only encounter several hundred people. The weeks around holy days of the year tend to have a higher pilgrim population: All Saints, Christmas, Easter, Ascension and Pentecost.[1] The more people there are in the community the busier the day appears. The lines are longer for food and at Oyak. It's harder to get a hot shower and find a place in the church. On the other hand, there are more people to meet during the summer months, the energy level is higher, and despite what you might think, the crowds in the church are significant in experiencing the ecumenical nature of the prayers.

When the pilgrim population is lower, however, it's possible to see the inner workings of the pilgrim community. You might be responsible for more than one job as the shared work demands. The pace of life in Taizé seems to slow down a bit. Additionally, you might find yourself in a sharing group or a work team with fewer English-speaking pilgrims. The lines are also shorter and the showers are warmer—which is not to say that those facets carry much weight in the grand scheme of the week. In short, both high- and low-populated times of the year have advantages and disadvantages. You'll have to determine the best time of the year for your visit.

When should I arrive in the community?

Although you can arrive in the community whenever your schedule dictates, if you're going to stay for a week, you should really plan on arriving on Sunday afternoon and leaving the following Sunday around noon. Granted, flights and transportation schedules don't always accommodate this schedule, so don't hold it as a mandatory stipulation. The reason Sunday is the ideal day to arrive, though, is that each week in Taizé carries with it a rhythm of its own. Sunday is the day when 95 percent of the pilgrims check in. Everyone is placed into work teams and decides what Bible Introductions they will attend for the week. If you arrive in the middle of the week, you will still be placed in a work team, however, your jobs might be more miscellaneous tasks that need accomplishing rather than a consistent job for the week. Another disadvantage of coming midweek, especially if you're planning to stay over a Sunday, is that Sunday can be a disjointed day in the community.

The Sunday morning prayers don't begin until 10:00 a.m., and most pilgrims are packing up their personal belongings before it begins. Backpacks are scattered throughout the community from both those departing and new pilgrims arriving. Also, there are no midday prayers on Sunday in order to prepare for the arrival of the coming week's visitors. Typically, if you are staying through a Sunday, you will be expected to help orient the new pilgrims to the community in some fashion. Furthermore, you will be reassigned a new dorm room, despite the fact that you've already settled into one. Practically speaking, this means if you've arrived on Thursday and are planning on leaving on the following Wednesday, you will experience the end of one week, then be welcomed again, given a new dorm room and assigned to a new work team for the new week. For these reasons, if it's at all possible avoid coming midweek, unless you're only staying for a few days.

TRANSPORTATION: PLANES, TRAINS AND BUSES

How do I get to Taizé?
There are many different ways of traveling to Taizé. None of them are easy, so if your question seeks simplicity, I'm not sure you're going to like my answer. Moreover, if you're traveling from the U.K. or another European country, please adjust the following directions accordingly. As I have only traveled to Taizé from the United States, I can only confidently offer my advice from that vantage point.

Transportation options vary greatly depending on whether or not you're bringing a group or traveling as an individual (or with just a friend or two).

No matter how you travel to the community, it will involve planes and buses; if you're traveling alone it will definitely include trains. The best way to answer the question is to walk with you along each step of the trip and give you the options that each step offers.

Traveling in a larger group has the potential to reduce the overall transportation points, however, it will require you to do a bit more legwork than I'm going to offer you in this description. If you're leading a group from the United States, it's not unreasonable to have each participant meet at the airport through their own means. If you're taking young people, many of the parents will want to see their kids off at the airport, so this could eliminate having to coordinate this leg of the transportation.

Your flight destination should be one of three airports: Paris Charles de Gaulle, Geneva International Airport or Lyon Saint-Exupery Airport. These three airports offer you the most options for traveling to Taizé. Of course, transatlantic flights often make several connections in various places across Europe before depositing you in your desired destination; when flying with a group through the night, the fewer of these connections you have to make the better.

If you have a group of at least forty people, my suggestion is to fly into Paris and rent a coach. This option will save you the confusion of connecting points and will keep everyone informed and together. You can arrange for the coach to pick you up from the airport and take you directly to Taizé. Although it will cost you a bit more, it might be worth the expense. Don't try this mode of transportation if your group is smaller, though, because it will raise the overall price of your trip dramatically.

If your group is between twelve and forty participants, I would suggest taking the train. Although you may have a few extra connection points, it will allow you to see a bit of the French countryside during the journey (that is, if you can stay awake). From Charles de Gaulle you'll want to take the Air France shuttle bus to the Gare de Lyon station in Paris. The shuttle ride lasts about an hour and drops you off right in front of the station. Then you'll need to make a round-trip group purchase for everyone to Mâcon-Loché. Although the return ticket can be altered, plan on returning to Paris between 1:00 p.m. and 3:00 p.m. (depending on if you're flying out that day or staying in Paris for a night or two) the following Sunday afternoon. This will give you plenty of time to make your way to Mâcon and get into Paris before nightfall. The total train time is about two hours. If you miss a train, however, the next high-speed TGV train may not leave for another two or three hours. It's worth looking up the train times on the Taizé website before you begin your journey.

From Mâcon you'll need to catch a bus to Taizé. The bus will drop you off right in front of Casa. Depending on the train times, the whole trip shouldn't last more than five or six hours from the time your plane lands to the time you're in the community. For more detailed, step-by-step instructions, see the Taizé website (http://www.taize.fr/en). All things considered, taking the train and the buses should run you about two hundred dollars per person round trip. It might seem like a hefty price, but considering the multiple modes of transportation and the remote location of Taizé, it's quite reasonable.

If you're traveling in a small group or as an individual, I would suggest a slightly different path. Rather than flying into Paris, I'd recommend flying into Lyon, which doesn't usually cost much more. It will most likely add one more connecting flight to your trip—often through Paris, Frankfurt or Milan—and thus make the flight portion of your journey a little longer. I've discovered, though, that once I leave the airport I want the rest of the journey to be as quick as possible, and Lyon is just about an hour south of Taizé (although it takes longer than an hour to get there). From Lyon, a shuttle bus will take you to Lyon Part Dieu. This bus ride lasts about thirty-five minutes. Once there you'll need to purchase a train ticket to Taizé via Mâcon (approximately twenty euros). After the short thirty-minute train ride to Mâcon, you'll probably meet up with the other Taizé-bound travelers boarding the local bus to Taizé. The bus ride from Mâcon to Taizé shouldn't take more than fifty minutes.

One factor to consider when deciding whether to fly into Paris or Lyon is whether or not you or your small group wants to spend some time in Paris. If you want to tack a sightseeing tour of Paris onto your trip, you should definitely fly into Charles de Gaulle. I'd suggest that you do that part of the trip first. Fly into Paris, take the shuttle bus to Gare de Lyon and then find a local hostel (there are plenty of them to choose from). Spend a few days touring the city and then make your way to Taizé on Sunday morning. To do this you'd need to leave on a Wednesday or Thursday prior to the week you want to spend in Taizé. Sightseeing after going to Taizé often defeats the purpose of going to the community. Pilgrims who visited Paris after their trip to Taizé lamented this order, as much of the thoughtfulness and contemplative spirit with which they departed the community was dampened by the hustle and bustle of the Parisian culture. Furthermore, touring the French capital directly before going to a simple monastic community could prove to be a good teaching moment for many pilgrims. To see the wealth, busyness and secular nature of Paris first only makes the communal life at Taizé more pronounced.

One final thought on transportation is worth mentioning. Remember that flying around certain holidays and anytime between late May and early September will result in a heftier price tag for your flight. When I went once in the summer, my ticket was over nine hundred dollars. Compare that with my off-season flight, which cost less than six hundred dollars. The price difference is significant and makes it worth doing some research before purchasing tickets. When do you want to go? How busy can you handle it? If six thousand people is a lot for you, perhaps you should consider a less busy time.

As I said in the beginning of the book, there is no easy way to get to Taizé. It will take many hours, most of which you will be utterly exhausted (flying through the night has that effect). But in the end, no pilgrimage should be easy. I sincerely believe that part of the transformation that takes place in Taizé is tied to the journey over. While I would love to be closer to Taizé, I count the drudgery of the trip a part of my pilgrimage. As you plan your own trip or the trip for your group, try to keep this in mind.

PACKING

What should I pack?

If you're like me, the question "what should I pack?" has a tendency to haunt you before you take trips anywhere, and it seems the farther you go, the more you tend to stress about it. When going to Taizé, however, I like to recommend this mindset: Think camping. Toss out the American notion of "more is better" and think minimalism. You really don't need much at Taizé. Remember, it's a monastery. One of the essential characteristics that personifies the lives of the brothers is simplicity. Thinking with this mindset *before* the trip helps prepare us for what God has in store. With that said, let me provide a basic list of items that will minimize your baggage and maximize your trip.

For clothing, you don't need "church clothes" during the week but you should think in terms of modesty. Bare shoulders are one of the few restrictions in the Church of Reconciliation. If you're wearing a tank top during the hot summer days, there is a box at the back of the church with some makeshift "shawls" which you can use to cover up your shoulders. Shorts are acceptable throughout the day when it's hot, although you do see more people in jeans and trousers during the evening prayers. Try to bring **clothing you can layer.** The weather is often unpredictable, and it's better to bring something to keep you dry than to have wet clothing all week. Also, keep in mind that Europeans wear clothing again more frequently than Americans. Don't be surprised if you see a person wearing the same shirt and trousers for three or four days straight. If you embrace this ideal for the week, it will significantly lighten your load. One of the weeks I was there, I wore the same pair of jeans the whole week and saved my one clean pair of chinos for the journey home. There are no laundry machines in Taizé for the larger pilgrim community; rest assured, though, if a plague of frogs or something soils the whole of your wardrobe, you could do laundry in the neighboring town of Cluny. Mind you, it's outrageously expensive—around twelve dollars per load—but if something tragic happened, this is a possibility.

As far as sleeping gear goes, plan to bring a **sleeping sack** or **sleeping bag** and a **travel pillow.** If you're traveling alone during the less-busy months, you might be able to get away with using one of the leftover sleeping bags or pillows in the community. Over the years, pilgrims have left their sleeping bags, blankets and pillows which are available for use, but they're available on a first come, first served basis. On my second trip to the community, I decided to forgo my sleeping gear, and while I ended up with an extra sleeping bag, I was *sans* pillow for the week. (There is nothing like dirty laundry stuffed in an old T-shirt for a pillow.) So it's worth the nocturnal security to bring your own. If you're taking a group, no matter what time of year, insist that everyone bring their own sleeping gear. All transatlantic flights allow for two check-ins, and the sleeping gear can count for the second.

You will need all your own **toiletries:** toothbrush, toothpaste, soap, shampoo, deodorant, etc. Also, don't forget to bring a **towel** and **shower shoes.** If you bring anything electronic for grooming (e.g., electric razor, hair dryer), make sure they work with a 220V current. A simple **travel adapter** attached to the end of your hair-dryer plug won't convert the powerful 220V current down to 110V; rather, it actually allows the current to flow into the appliance. In other words, if your razor, hair dryer or flat iron won't take a 220V current, don't bring it along. If you do have appliances that can take a 220V current, all you need to use those items is a simple travel adapter. If you do forget a basic toiletry item, remember you can always pick up a few essentials at Oyak. The little shop (called the Bazaar) stocks toothbrushes, toothpaste, shampoo, soap, feminine products, tissues and other similar items.

Naturally, you'll want to bring your **Bible,** a **notepad,** and a **pen or pencil.** Although you won't need any of these items in the prayers (since the Scriptures are printed on handouts), these items will be helpful in the Bible Introductions, especially if you're the only English-speaking pilgrim there during a less-busy week. The pen and paper will definitely come in handy for recording all the addresses and emails of your newfound friends (just like camp!).

One item you'll appreciate having in the prayers is a **prayer stool.** It's usually small enough to pack in your backpack, or you can just carry it under your arm or strap it to your carry-on. If bringing one seems bothersome, the brothers sell prayer stools for around twenty-five dollars in the Exposition. They're not hard to construct if you're so inclined. Either way, I'd recommend having one while you're at Taizé. Despite the cumbersome nature of lugging it around, it will offer you more seating options in the church.

If you're ecofriendly you might also consider bringing a **reusable water bottle.** There are several places where you can fill your water bottles in the community. If you opt not to save the earth, however, you can always purchase both still and bubbly water from Oyak or from the vending machine. Like everything else at Oyak, water is inexpensive.

If you're planning on communicating with people in the United States while in Taizé, your best bet is to pick up an **international phone card,** or sign up for an international calling plan with your local carrier before you go. Alternatively, calling cards can be purchased at Taizé or in a kiosk at the train station before you get to the community, though you'll get more minutes for your money if you purchase one prior to your trip. Also, make sure you get an *international* card, unless you know a lot of people in France who you want to call. If you've got a codependent relationship with your cell phone, you might want to take a break from it, as international cell-phone rates are quite expensive and you'll be faced with the issue of how to charge the phone (see below). If you're on a phone plan that includes international text-messaging and email, though, it would definitely be worth taking the phone along. If you're taking a group, you'll need some way of communicating with the home base, whether it's a church, school or organization. The best advice I can give you is to figure it out beforehand; otherwise you might find yourself with a hefty phone bill.

The issue of how to get money is always a popular question. The first and easiest way is to bring a **bankcard** with you and simply withdraw whatever you need from a French ATM. While it's the most convenient method because you can get cash when you need it, it does come with a nice little "gift" on your bank statement once the trip is over. In my experience, the bank charge for these transactions can be up to fifteen dollars per withdrawal, which includes both the bank commission and the transaction fee from your bank. Depending on your bank's ATM policy, this still might be the best option. **Credit cards** are also one of the most convenient ways to pay for your purchases while overseas. The community accepts both MasterCard and Visa for the room-and-board charges and all of your purchases in the Exposition. Another viable option is to bring euros with you. You can obtain euros from your bank before your departure, but don't wait until the last minute, as most banks don't stock euros on a daily basis. The drawback of this option is that you'll probably still face a charge from your bank for the transaction (depending on the type of account you hold). Moreover, if you need extra cash, you'll still need to use a bankcard or credit card.

If all else fails you can also bring U.S. dollars. These can be exchanged for euros at most exchange booths in the airport or at major train stations. Note, however, that the exchange rate you get from these booths is usually worse than you would get from a bank, especially if they claim to not charge a commission (that means they're robbing you enough in the exchange). Having U.S. dollars is an especially good last-minute option if you're running out of money. When you purchase something in dollars in the Exposition, they will give you back change in euros. Using a twenty-dollar bill to pay for something as simple as a thirty-five-cent postcard, for example, will yield ample spending money for snacks at Oyak. On one trip to Taizé, I forgot my bankcard PIN, which left me with a few euros I had saved from my last trip and my credit cards to pay for everything. While I used my credit card for my transportation to Taizé and to cover my room and board, I didn't have much cash left over to buy my interviewees hot drinks at Oyak. By purchasing postcards at the Exposition, I was able to survive the week without much difficulty (and send a lot of postcards in the process).

Another item you'll definitely want to remember is your **camera.** In addition to snapping a few photos of the community's grounds, you'll meet plenty of new friends you'll want to remember long after your memories begin to fade. Disposable cameras can also be purchased at Oyak if need be. One word about the cameras, though: please do not take pictures during the prayer times. The brothers frown on this activity and so do many of the pilgrims. While for some visitors Taizé may seem a bit like a tourist attraction, for most it's a holy place. Camera flashes and video cameras are sure to evoke stern faces and reprimands in other languages. Trust me, I've seen it happen many times. With that in mind, I'll highlight a few items you might want to leave behind, especially if you're creating a packing list for a student group.

Though you might be tempted to bring all your electronic devices along with you, even if only for the plane ride, there are a few things you may want to consider when choosing what to pack. First, electrical outlets are few and far between at Taizé. Outside the dormitories there are only a few electrical outlets, which are often being used to charge cell phones, and there are no outlets inside the dorm rooms. If you're lucky, you might have a dorm room situated directly next to an outlet, but if that's the case you should expect a crowd of people milling around your door at all hours of the night waiting for their phones and MP3 players to charge. Although some people leave their phones plugged in and come back for them later, it's not uncommon for a phone or PDA to be unplugged and left on the ground or even stolen (it's happened once to my knowledge in the few times I've stayed in the dormitories). If you've got a cell phone, MP3 player, PDA or laptop that you feel you must bring with you, keep in mind that your charging options are limited to the bathroom shaver outlets and the few outlets on the exterior of the dormitories. None of these options is really worth the hassle, and there isn't a WiFi signal for miles, so if you're an email junky, you might want to think about using your time in Taizé to fast from it! I've had to bring my laptop with me due to my research, and it's always been a pain having to sit around and wait for it to charge—definitely something I would prefer to do without. Moreover, as I stated earlier in the book, the doors of the dormitories are only locked during the prayers, so unless you're keen on hauling your expensive electronic devices around with you for the week, I'd leave them at home. In the end, bring what you absolutely need, and nothing more.

One final thought on packing: If you have a larger backpack available, it's advisable to use that over a standard suitcase. With the multiple connection points and having to get on and off different modes of transportation, you'll be thankful you're traveling with something you can throw on your back. If your back won't take a forty-pound pack then consider a rolling duffle. They tend to be narrower than your standard rectangular suitcase and easier to maneuver. Also, don't forget to leave some room for a few purchases from the Exposition. The brothers make beautiful pottery and have an array of other items you'll want to stow away for the return journey. Although pottery is a pain to travel with, once you're home you'll be delighted you went to the trouble.

The *Side* Trip

Are there other historical sites to see near Taizé?
Despite the fact that the brothers discourage leaving the village for day trips, many pilgrims get a bit antsy midweek and decide to grab a bus to one of the local villages. Cormatin is a little village within walking distance of the community. During the hot summer afternoons, you can often see a little trail of Taizé visitors making their way through Ameugny and down the winding roads of the Burgundy countryside. Cormatin doesn't lay claim to much, but there are a few cafés where a strong cup of espresso and a French pastry can be purchased.

Another popular destination is the quaint town of Cluny, one of the most significant cities in the development of Western monasticism. Cluny boasts more than historical significance, however, as it offers the tourist all the conveniences of a much larger city. Within the city walls you'll find restaurants, cafés, a small grocery store, a French patisserie, an SNCF agency (which is the French National Railway Company and is where you will need to go if your train tickets need to be adjusted) and many other boutiques in the town's center.

While these outings can be enjoyable, I've found that remaining in the village is essential to experiencing the fullness of communal life. When pilgrims remove themselves from the daily schedule of the community, they are inevitably missing something—their work, a sharing time or perhaps the midday prayers. While it might not seem too damaging to miss one component for an afternoon, it has a greater effect than people realize. When pilgrims leave the community, they essentially are saying that their needs—whether they are tourist reasons or a simple desire to have a real cup of coffee—are greater than the community's need to function as a whole. While their absence might not bankrupt the discussion of a sharing group or prohibit a work team from completing its task, it does send a message that seems rather antithetical to what Taizé is really about. Unfortunately, sometimes it does dramatically affect other pilgrims.

Imagine being placed on a work team whose sole job was to clean the bathrooms at Oyak. If half the team decides one afternoon to head into Cluny, the burden of that decision falls on the shoulders of the few who remain in the community. Each week the brothers host thousands of young people with the expectation that they will join in the daily rhythm of their communal life. Leaving the community for personal reasons, justified as they may be, does affect how the pilgrim community functions and ultimately how it perceives itself.

That said, visitors will continue to take these side trips during the week in Taizé. The brothers don't enforce their preference, as they want everyone to feel free to embrace the communal nature of Taizé at their own pace. As you plan your own trip or establish guidelines for your group, take this aspect of the community into consideration.

While some of the above information may seem superfluous with a pilgrimage to Taizé still in its conceptual stage, hopefully on the eve of your trip this appendix will prove to be a resource and a reminder of what you might need, rather than a checklist for everything you must take with you.

When you're packing for your trip, there is one final "thing" everyone should remember to bring with them: an expectant spirit. Ephesians 3:20 reminds us that God is able to do abundantly above all that we can ever ask or think. When planning a trip to Taizé, expect great things from God, and let his grace, peace and love overwhelm you.

CONSOLIDATED PACKING LIST

- ATM bankcard and credit card
- Bible
- Camera (film, batteries, memory cards)
- Clothing you can layer
- International phone card
- Notepad
- Pen or pencil
- Prayer stool or cushion
- Reusable water bottle
- Shower shoes
- Sleeping bag or sack
- Toiletries
- Towel
- Travel adapter
- Travel pillow

Appendix B

The Life Commitment

☙

Beloved brother, what are you asking for?

The mercy of God and the community of my brothers.

May God complete in you what he has begun.

Brother, you trust in God's mercy: remember that the Lord Christ comes to help the weakness of your faith; committing himself with you, he fulfills for you his promise:

Truly, there is no one who has left everything because of Christ and the gospel who will not receive a hundred times as much at present—brothers and sisters and mothers and children—and persecutions too, and in the age to come eternal life (Mark 10:29-30 and Luke 18:29-30).

This is a way contrary to all human reason; you can only advance along it by faith, not by sight (2 Corinthians 5:7), always sure that whoever gives their life for Christ's sake will find it (Matthew 16:25).

From now on walk in the steps of Christ. Do not be anxious about tomorrow (Matthew 6:34). First, seek God's Kingdom and its justice (Matthew 6:33). Surrender yourself, give yourself, and good measure, pressed down, shaken together, brimming over, will be poured out for you.

Whether you walk or sleep, night and day the seed springs up and grows, you do not know how (Mark 4:27).

Avoid making sure you are noticed by others to gain their admiration (Matthew 6:1). Never let your inner life make you look sad, like a hypocrite who puts on a grief-stricken air to attract attention. Anoint your head and wash your face, so that only your Father who is in secret knows what your heart intends (Matthew 6:16-18).

Stay simple and full of joy, the joy of the merciful, the joy of brotherly love.

Be vigilant. If you have to rebuke a brother, keep it between the two of you (Matthew 18:15).

Be concerned to establish communion with your neighbor.

Be open about yourself, remembering that you have a brother whose charge it is to listen to you. Bring him your understanding so that he can fulfill his ministry with joy (Hebrews 13:17).

The Lord Christ, in his compassion and his love for you, has chosen you to be in the Church, a sign of brotherly love. It is his will that with your brothers you live the parable of community.

So, refusing to look back (Philippians 3:13), and joyful with infinite gratitude, never fear to rise to meet the dawn (Psalm 119:147),

praising

blessing

and singing

Christ your Lord.

Receive me, Lord Christ, and I will live; may my expectation be a source of joy.

Brother, remember that it is Christ who calls you and that it is to him that you are now going to respond.

Will you, for love of Christ, consecrate yourself to him with all your being?

I will.

Will you henceforth fulfill your service of God within our community, in communion with your brothers?

I will.

Will you, renouncing all ownership, live with your brothers not only in community of material goods but also in community of spiritual goods, in utter openness of heart?

I will.

Will you, in order to be more available to serve with your brothers, and in order to give yourself in undivided love to Christ, remain in celibacy?

I will.

Will you, so that we may be of one heart and one mind and so that the unity of our common service may be fully achieved, adopt the orientations of the community expressed by the prior, bearing in mind that he is a poor servant within the community?

I will.

Will you, always discerning Christ in your brothers, watch over them in good days and bad, in suffering and in joy?

I will.

In consequence, because of Christ and the gospel, you are henceforth a brother of our community.

May this ring be the sign of our fidelity in the Lord.[1]

Appendix C

Resources

Selected Books

Brico, Rex. *Taizé: Brother Roger and His Community.* Glasgow: William Collins, Sons, 1978.

Brother Roger of Taizé. *The Sources of Taizé: No Greater Love.* Chicago: GIA Publications, 2000.

Brother Roger of Taizé and Marcello Fidanzio. *Brother Roger of Taizé: Essential Writings.* New York: Orbis, 2006.

Carey, George. *Spiritual Journey: 1,000 Young Adults Share the Reconciling Experience of Taizé with the Archbishop of Canterbury.* Harrisburg, Penn.: Morehouse Publishing, 1994.

Clément, Oliver. *Taizé: A Meaning to Life.* Chicago: GIA Publications, 1997.

González-Balado, José Luis. *The Story of Taizé.* New York: Seabury Press, 1981.

Spink, Kathryn. *A Universal Heart: The Life and Vision of Brother Roger of Taizé.* 2nd ed. Chicago: GIA Publications, 2005.

Taizé Community. *Seeds of Trust: Reflecting on the Bible in Silence and Song.* Harrisburg, Penn.: Morehouse Publishing, 2005.

Taizé Community. *Taizé: Songs for Prayer.* Chicago: GIA Publications, 1998.

WEBSITES

http://www.taize.fr/en

This is the Taizé community's main website. If this book fails to answer all your questions, you should be able to find answers here.

http://www.sncf.fr

This is the website for the Société Nationale des Chemins de fer Français, or in English, the French National Railway Company. Once at the site, simply click the little Great Britain flag in the upper right corner to access the English version of the site. (Or, if you prefer to type the URL address: http://sncf.fr/index.php?LANG=en_EN.)

http://www.giamusic.com

This site is great for ordering Taizé resources in North America. Click on "Composers/Authors/Artists" and then on "Taizé Community" for a list of available resources.

Glossary

El Abiodh. Pronounced "el ah-bee-ohd," this building, whose name literally means "the white" in Arabic, was named not only because of its color but more importantly after a place in the Sahara desert where a monastic community, the Little Brothers of Jesus, live. It was built in 1965 as Taizé's first guesthouse for the community. Today, the community continues to host pilgrims in El Abiodh's small rooms, although they reserve these accommodations for older visitors, the brother's families and those with special needs. In the colder months, pilgrims can borrow extra blankets, sleeping sacks and camping pads from El Abiodh—so long as they haven't run out.

Ameugny. Ameugny is a neighboring village about a half-mile from the Church of Reconciliation. In addition to the house where the Sisters of St. Andrew live, the family housing area, called Olinda, is located here.

assembly. In Taizé, the assembly refers to the seating area in the Church of Reconciliation. The term also designates the gathering of people present in the church at any given time.

barrack. *Barrack* is the term the brothers use for their dormitory style accommodations. In total, the barracks can sleep around two thousand people. Each room can accommodate between eight to ten people.

Bible Introductions. Bible Introductions are daily Bible study meetings that take place before noon Monday through Saturday. During the busier weeks, several different topics are offered. Most Bible Introductions take place in the Church of Reconciliation (except during the weeks when the adults and families have separate gatherings).

Casa. *Casa,* which literally means "house" in Spanish, functions as Taizé's official welcome house. It's the building where all visitors and pilgrims check into the community. At Casa, pilgrims can get meal cards, room assignments, and schedules for buses and trains.

choir, the. Historically, the "choir" was often the area between the nave and the chancel where the choir would occasionally sing. In Taizé, however, there is no proper choir, yet the brothers have continued to call the whole area "the choir."

Church of Reconciliation. Designed by Brother Denis and completed in 1962 with the help of a German organization called Aktion Sühnezeichen, which selected Taizé's building project to offer a sign of peace to France. (*Süh-nezeichen,* which literally means "sign of atonement/reconciliation," was established in 1958 by Lothar Kreyssig to help rebuild the areas that were destroyed during the war.) In 1971, however, the back wall of the church—including the stained-glass window it held—was torn down to accommodate more young people. Several additions were added throughout the years to bring it to its current size, which holds around six thousand people.

Cluny. Located only a few kilometers from Taizé, Cluny once boasted the most prestigious and endowed monasteries in all of western Europe. The town is also known for the remains of the Cluny Abbey, which was founded on September 2, 909, by William I, count of Auvergne. Up to the sixteenth century, Cluny boasted the largest ecclesial edifice in Europe before the Vatican renovated St. Peter's Cathedral in Rome. In 1790, however, Cluny was attacked and destroyed during the French Revolution, and only fragments of the once great Cluny Cathedral remain.

Dynamic of the Provisional. The *Dynamic of the Provisional* is a book written in the early 1960s by Brother Roger (published in English in 1981 through Mowbray Press, Oxford). It refers to a way of living out the Christian life by being willing to consider the provisional nature of our calling and was written around the time when the Second Vatican Council was taking place. Essentially Brother Roger was asking the question, have we become too static in our thinking about the Christian life? The *Dynamic of the Provisional* challenges us to continually rethink how we conceptualize our particular expression of faith.

les Jeunes. A French word that means "the young," *les Jeunes* is a catchall term used by some of the brothers to refer to the young pilgrims in the community.

Lyon. The third largest city in France (coming after Paris and Marseilles, respectively). It is a major center of business and an ideal city to fly into in order to get to Taizé.

Mâcon. A medium-sized town located between Lyon and Taizé. Beautiful in its own right, it is the capital of the Saône-et-Loire area, in the Burgundy region of France. For pilgrims traveling to Taizé by train, Mâcon is the last stop before arriving in the community. After taking a train to one of Mâcon's three train stations, travelers must take a bus to finish their journey to the community.

La Morada. La Morada is a building that sits adjacent to Casa (the welcome center). It functions as a gateway to the brothers. La Morada was first named "Tyniec" after a Benedictine monastery in Cracow, Poland. Brother Roger, however, felt that it was too difficult to pronounce, so they changed it to "The Yellow House." It was called the Yellow House for many years, but even though it was an accurate description of the building, it seemed to "lack something." Thus its name was eventually changed to La Morada, which means "the dwelling" in Spanish. Today, most pilgrims visit La Morada to deposit and then retrieve their valuables.

Olinda. Olinda is the family housing area owned by the community. It's located in Ameugny, only a half-mile from the Church of Reconciliation. In addition to sleeping accommodations, Olinda offers meeting tents and a small playground for children.

Oyak. Oyak is Taizé's only concession area where pilgrims can purchase drinks, snacks and personal items. It officially opened in the early 1980s and was named after a town in Cameroon, near the large port city of Douala. Selling all its goods at cost, Oyak is a popular gathering place for conversation and fellowship during certain periods of the day and after evening prayers.

permanents. While in English the term *permanent* means "lasting or unchanged," in French, *les permanent* literally means "a union, party official, or worker," conveying the notion of a paid administrative member of a staff. Ironically, neither really captures the essence of permanents at Taizé. Permanents are not long-term residents at Taizé and they're not paid workers. They are, in a word, volunteers—young people who live for a determined period in the community to help organize the larger pilgrim population. They are not officially part of the Brothers of Taizé, although many young men consider what it would be like to be a brother during their tenure as permanents.

sharing groups. Sharing groups at Taizé are similar to small groups or cell groups. Depending on the national makeup of the week, the sharing groups are divided by languages and ages. The aim of these student-led small groups is to encourage discussion about the biblical text that was used during the Bible Introduction.

Sisters of St. Andrew. The Sisters of St. Andrew are a medieval order dating back almost eight hundred years. Their home base is in Tournai, Belgium, from which they support dozens of satellite groups of sisters ministering in various capacities around the world. Noted for their connection to the mystical spirituality of St. Ignatius of Loyola, they have established a location in Ameugny, a neighboring village of Taizé. The sisters have assisted the Brothers of Taizé with the female pilgrims and permanents since the mid 1960s.

Source of Saint Steven. Saint Steven's Source (La Source de Saint Etienne) is a wooded area filled with winding paths that lead down to a lake complete with a bubbling brook, a small waterfall and a charming little bridge over the water. Although the hours for the Source are limited, it's a treasure at Taizé that many visitors overlook.

TGV. TGV stands for *train à grande vitesse,* which translates into "high-speed train" in English. The TGVs are operated by SNCF (French National Railway Company). Beginning in 1981 with a high-speed passage from Lyon to Paris, TGVs now reach many other corners of France using Paris as their central hub. It holds the record for the fastest wheeled train, reaching 357 miles per hour (574.8 kilometers per hour) on April 3, 2007. If you're coming from Paris, a TGV is the fastest way to Mâcon.

Acknowledgments

As I consider all the people who played a role in the formation of this book, I find myself extremely grateful for the community of friends and family who surround me. The following list is sure to leave out a number of people whose conversations helped form many of my thoughts and assertions contained in this book. Most notable are the young people (and former young people) who took the time to converse with me over a cup of coffee or beer in Taizé. My hope is that in this project I have represented their search for God with integrity. To all of you, thank you for enriching my understanding of the Taizé community.

It probably goes without saying, but if it weren't for the Brothers of Taizé, this book would have never materialized. While there are many brothers who contributed to my research through interviews, emails and casual conversation, two walked with me in seeing this project from its inception to its final form. Thank you, Brother John and Brother Emile, for trusting me to represent your community to English-speaking audiences across the globe. You will probably never know the impact your trust has made on me. I truly hope the fruits of my labor encourage you, as you trust other young people to share your passion for reconciliation.

I would also like to thank the good people at InterVarsity Press, and specifically my editor, David Zimmerman, for trusting an unknown doctoral student with this book. Dave is an avid comic-book fan and writer whose "super power" is clearly making the story that you just read more intelligible. Although he swears none of his other authors call him late at night at his home, I know he's just saying that to be funny. I thank God for your wisdom, your humor and your friendship, Dave; you have been a sustaining force in making this experience educational and rewarding.

I would also like to thank my professors and colleagues at Princeton Theological Seminary: Richard Osmer, Kenda Creasy Dean, Gordon Mikoski, Bo Karen Lee, Darrell Guder, Drew Dyson, Andrew Zirschky and Amanda Drury. In particular, I would like to thank my adviser, Kenda Creasy Dean, who despite her reservations about me writing this book in the middle of a Ph.D. program, supported me through her mentorship and endless stream of encouraging words.

There were also many conversation partners whose insight helped form the initial shape of this book. Thank you, Nate Phillips, Doug Zimmerman and Lisa O'Reilly, for your willingness to read my rough drafts in the early stages of my writing. I would also like to thank those who helped fund my research trips to Taizé: Carol Kloster, Brent LeGris, Charlie and Eileen Jacobs, Mom and Dad, the American Protestant Church, and the Lily Foundation. Your generosity has enabled me to share an important story that needed to be told.

Finally, I would like to thank my wife, Shannon, and my son, Judah, who have given me more support than they'll ever realize. Not only did Shannon endure far too many verbal brainstorming sessions about Taizé (it's a wonder she still likes the community), she has always been my first editor, making sure my silly mistakes and typos aren't aired for all to see. Your love and friendship are among the most precious gifts I have ever known. And to my son, Judah, thank you for allowing Daddy to write when I know that more than anything, you just wanted me to play with you. You're an amazing son and I hope that my efforts here will have a lasting effect on your understanding of God, the church and the hope we have in our Savior, Jesus Christ.

Notes

❧

CHAPTER 1: MY PILGRIMAGE TO TAIZÉ
[1] The epigraphs throughout the book are from the Taizé Songbook.

CHAPTER 2: WELCOME TO TAIZÉ
[1] If you really want the full experience of traveling from North America to Taizé as you read this chapter, follow these simple instructions: (1) Put the book down right now. (2) Stay up all night sitting in a small uncomfortable chair. Eat a microwave dinner in your lap around 1:00 a.m. (If you have a video iPod or portable DVD player, feel free to watch movies on the little screen.) (3) At the crack of dawn, go ride on the public transportation (buses and trains) in your local town or city. (4) Then at about noon, come back to the book and continue reading.

[2] English translation: "My home is your home."

[3] Depending on the number of pilgrims in Taizé, your welcome may be in another area around Casa. Adults and families, for instance, are welcomed in a meeting room about fifty yards from the front of Casa.

[4] During the beginning of the twentieth century, the Frenchman Charles de Foucauld lived a life of prayer while ministering to Muslims. His influence in the area inspired the creation of two communities: the Little Brothers of Jesus and the Little Sisters of Jesus.

[5] Permanents are young people who live for a determined period in the community to help organize the larger pilgrim population. They are not officially part of the Taizé community, although many young men consider becoming a brother during their tenure as permanents.

CHAPTER 4: BROTHER ROGER AND THE FORMATION OF A COMMUNITY
[1] This chapter only offers a condensed look at Taizé's history, with an emphasis on the early

years. It aims to frame for you an overarching perspective on the development of the community and is in no way exhaustive in its detail or scope. Although I have conducted my own extensive research with the brothers, I must give credit to those authors who have contributed to my own understanding of Taizé's history. Some of the historical accounts I present are enhanced by the research of these writers. If you find the community's history intriguing and desire a more detailed account, I would suggest the following authors: First, Rex Brico, a Dutch-born, naturalized British journalist and playwright who chronicles the life of the community up to the late 1970s. His book *Taizé: Brother Roger and His Community* (Glasgow: William Collins, Sons, 1978) is the basis from which many articles and books have been written. Moreover, it contains a wonderful collection of pictures from the earlier years of the community. Second, José Luis González-Balado's book *The Story of Taizé* (New York: Seabury Press, 1981) has become perhaps the most-resourced English account of Taizé's history. First published in Spanish and then in English in 1980, this little book is equally informative and accessible. It too, however, only records the history of the community up to the late 1970s. Finally, the British biographer Kathryn Spink also traces the development of the Taizé community in what is the most extensive English account of Brother Roger's life to date. Originally published in 1986, *A Universal Heart: The Life and Vision of Brother Roger of Taizé,* 2nd ed. (Chicago: GIA Publications, 2005) offers an in-depth look at the significance of Brother Roger's life in the growth of the Taizé community and in ecumenism worldwide. Of the three, Spink's book is the most readily available today. Brico's and González-Balado's books might require a little more hunting, as they are both currently out of print. Whether your interest in Taizé's history ends after reading this chapter or whether you scour the Internet and locate the other three English accounts, one thing is certain—you are about to read about the history and development of a community whose very existence was, and continues to be, defined by an unremitting desire to live out the gospel and bring Christ's reconciliation to the world.

[2]Although another child was born after Roger, the baby did not survive (Spink, *Universal Heart,* p. 4).

[3]Ibid.

[4]Ibid., p. 19.

[5]González-Balado, *Story of Taizé,* p. 28.

[6]Originally, the "third order" was a group of people who lived according to the third rule of Saint Francis of Assisi. While his first order was for monks and the second for nuns, the third order was comprised of laypeople who commonly lived outside of a religious community. Today, however, the term *third order* typically includes all lay members of religious orders who don't live in the community.

[7]González-Balado, *Story of Taizé,* p. 28.

[8]In the years that followed, La Grande Communauté would gather in Taizé for retreats and special gatherings. Roger returned to the university as he was able. In 1950, after several brothers had joined Roger in Taizé, the members of La Grande Communauté decided that

the two communities should make a permanent break.

[9]Brico, *Taizé,* pp. 14, 15.

[10]Ibid., p. 19 (italics mine).

[11]Spink, *Universal Heart,* p. 62.

[12]During an interview with one of the brothers, it was clear that there were past misunderstandings surrounding the North American conception of "fraternity" and the French use of the word. While it may seem obvious to some readers, these "fraternities" should not be confused with a North American understanding of fraternities and the collegiate Greek system. The fraternities established by the brothers were characterized by a common life similar to the way the brothers in Taizé live—common work and property, prayer three times a day, etc.—not by parties and binge drinking!

[13]Brother Roger of Taizé, *The Sources of Taizé: No Greater Love* (Chicago: GIA Publications, 2000).

[14]Spink, *Universal Heart,* p. 73.

CHAPTER 5: A NEW ERA OF RECONCILIATION

[1]Kathryn Spink, *A Universal Heart: The Life and Vision of Brother Roger of Taizé,* 2nd ed. (Chicago: GIA Publications, 2005), p. 79.

[2]José Luis González-Balado, *The Story of Taizé* (New York: Seabury Press, 1981), p. 66.

[3]Rex Brico, *Taizé: Brother Roger and His Community* (Glasgow: William Collins, Sons, 1978), p. 32.

[4]Ibid. It's worth noting that in French, *concile,* which is translated "council" in English, is used only for the solemn church assemblies, for example, the famous councils of church history like the Council of Constantinople. When Brother Roger announced a *Concile des Jeunes* five years after the Council of Vatican II, the ecclesial nature was obvious because of the term "council."

[5]Kathryn Spink, *Mother Teresa: A Complete Authorized Biography* (New York: HarperCollins, 1997), pp. 152-53.

CHAPTER 6: THE BROTHERS OF TAIZÉ

[1]The brothers set up Operation Hope, a nonprofit charity that aids those who are poor and afflicted around the world. In past years, Operation Hope has assisted in various nations, including (but not limited to) North Korea (donated 1,000 tons of corn and 1,000 tons of wheat flour), Ethiopia (AIDS relief), Philippines (assisted in rebuilding after typhoons), Burkina Faso (drilled wells for clean drinking water) and China (set up libraries for church parishes).

CHAPTER 8: THE PRAYERS OF TAIZÉ

[1]The name *Huguenot* originated in the mid-sixteenth century as a designation for members of the Protestant Reformed Church of France, which stems back to the great French reformer, John Calvin.

[2]Montserrat, which literally means "jagged mountain," became a pilgrimage site because a wooden statue of the black Madonna was discovered hidden in a cave. As the legend has it, the Benedictine monks, unwilling to move the Madonna, decided to build their monastery around the discovery site.

CHAPTER 9: THE HEART OF TAIZÉ

[1]Dietrich Bonhoeffer, *Life Together,* trans. John W. Doberstein (New York: HarperCollins, 1954), p. 26.

[2]While today the brothers do not typically call the pilgrims "guests," in the early years of the community visitors were often referred to that way. Brother Roger of Taizé, *The Rule of Taizé* (Taizé: Les Presses de Taizé, 1968), p. 115.

[3]Bonhoeffer, *Life Together,* p. 38.

[4]Taizé Community, *Seek and You Will Find: Questions on the Christian Faith and the Bible* (Harrisburg, Penn.: Morehouse Publishing, 2005), p. 55.

[5]Brother Roger, *Rule of Taizé,* p. 15.

[6]Ibid., p. 13.

CHAPTER 10: IMPORTING TAIZÉ

[1]See Christian Smith's *Soul Searching: The Religious and Spiritual Lives of American Teenagers* (New York: Oxford University Press, 2005); Robert Wuthnow's *After the Baby Boomers: How Twenty- and Thirty-Somethings Are Shaping the Future of American Religion* (Princeton, N.J.: Princeton University Press, 2007); and Mike Hayes's *Googling God: The Religious Landscape of People in Their 20s and 30s* (New York: Paulist Press, 2007).

[2]See Colleen Carroll's *The New Faithful: Why Young Adults Are Embracing Christian Orthodoxy* (Chicago: Loyola Press, 2002), and Thomas Oden's *The Rebirth of Orthodoxy: Signs of New Life in Christianity* (San Francisco: HarperSanFrancisco, 2003).

APPENDIX A: PRACTICAL ISSUES AND GETTING TO TAIZÉ

[1]During All Saints week, French schools bring their younger students in two shifts during the week (Sunday to Wednesday and Thursday to Sunday). It's the only time of the year when the Prayers around the Cross and the Vigil of Lights are celebrated twice. For the most part, these young people have never been to Taizé, so their presence creates a different environment in the community. For example, the prayers are filled with a bit more chatter than other weeks and the energy level overall is much higher.

APPENDIX B: THE LIFE COMMITMENT

[1]Brother Roger of Taizé, *The Sources of Taizé: No Greater Love* (Chicago: GIA Publications, 2000), pp. 72-74 (parenthetical Scripture references were originally formatted as endnotes).

formatio
TRADITION. EXPERIENCE.
TRANSFORMATION.

Formatio books from InterVarsity Press follow the rich tradition of the church in the journey of spiritual formation. These books are not merely about being informed, but about being transformed by Christ and conformed to his image. Formatio stands in InterVarsity Press's evangelical publishing tradition by integrating God's Word with spiritual practice and by prompting readers to move from inward change to outward witness. InterVarsity Press uses the chambered nautilus for Formatio, a symbol of spiritual formation because of its continual spiral journey outward as it moves from its center. We believe that each of us is made with a deep desire to be in God's presence. Formatio books help us to fulfill our deepest desires and to become our true selves in light of God's grace.